Study Guide to

Disgrace
by J. M. Coetzee

by Ray Moore

John Maxwell Coetzee in Warsaw (Poland) on June 7, 2006. The photograph was taken by Mariusz Kubik who has made it available for use. (Source: Wikimedia Commons.)

Copyright © Ray Moore 2017

Preface:

A Study Guide is an *aid* to the close reading of a text; it is *never* a substitute for reading the text. This novel deserves to be read *reflectively*, and the aim of this guide is to facilitate such a reading. The study guide questions have *no* answers provided. This is a deliberate choice. I am writing for readers who want to come to *their own conclusions* about the text and not simply to be told what to think about it by someone else. Even 'suggested' answers would limit the *exploration of the text* by readers themselves which is my primary aim.

In the classroom, I found that students frequently came up with answers that I had not even considered, and, not infrequently, that they expressed their ideas better than I could have done. The point of this Guide is to *open up* the text, not to close it down by providing 'ready-made answers.

Acknowledgements

As always, I am indebted to the work of many critics. Where I am conscious of having taken an idea or a phrase from a particular author, I cite the source in the text: failure to do so is an omission which I will immediately correct if it is drawn to my attention.

I believe that all quotations used in the book and other sources fall under the definition of 'fair use'. Once again, if I am in error on any quotation, I will immediately remove it if it is drawn to my attention. The image of a cat's cradle is in the public domain (source Wikimedia Commons),

Spoiler alert!

If you are reading the novel for the first time, you may wish to go straight to the Study Guide and Questions section and come back to the introductory sections later since they do explain what happens in the novel, including the ending

Contents

Introduction 1
Dramatis Personæ – A Selective List of Characters and Historical Figures 3
Genre 7
Narrative voice 8
Setting 9
Themes 10
    Rape 10
    Fathers and Daughters 12
    Animal and Humans 13
    Symbolism 14
    The Byron Opera 14
Study Guide: Translations, Questions and Commentary 16
Literary terms 62
Literary terms Activity 66
Appendix 1: How I Used the Study Guide Questions 68
Graphic Organizer- plot 70
To the Reader 71

Disgrace by J.M. Coetzee

Introduction

Plot Summary:

The narrative is set in post-apartheid South Africa. David Lurie, a twice-divorced, fifty-two-year-old adjunct Professor of Communications at Cape Technical University in Cape Town has an affair with one of his young female students. The young woman, or someone acting on her behalf, files a complaint for sexual harassment, and Lurie, who refuses publically to apologize for his actions, is dismissed from his post.

Leaving Cape Town, Lurie goes to stay with his daughter Lucy who owns a small farm (which Lurie bought for her) in the Eastern Cape where she also runs a boarding kennel. Lurie has all sorts of personal issues to work out with Lucy (not least that she is lesbian), but these are overshadowed by the increasing danger to isolated white farmers who are vulnerable to attack from some members of the black population resentful after years of racial, economic and political oppression.

One day, three black men approach the farm on the pretext of needing to use the telephone. What follows is a vicious attack and robbery in which the dogs are killed, Lurie is badly burned, and Lucy is raped. The police seem powerless to find the attackers, but Lucy consistently refuses to consider giving up her farm. Eventually, Lurie learns that his daughter is pregnant. Lucy insists on having the child despite everything Lurie says against it. Lurie now has to decide what to do – which really involves deciding who he is and what he values.

Why Read this Book?

The novel, which was published in 1999, won the Booker Prize. (Coetzee had already won the Booker in 1983 for his novel *Life and Times of Michael K.*) In 2003, the author was awarded the Nobel Prize in Literature. In 2006, the British newspaper *The Observer* asked 150 literary luminaries to vote for the best British, Irish or Commonwealth novel from 1980 to 2005: *Disgrace* topped the list! I probably would not go that far, but you have to respect the vote.

Disgrace was the last novel Coetzee published before emigrating to Australia in 2002.

Anyone interested in the recent history of South Africa would benefit from reading this novel. More fundamentally, anyone interested in exploring what it means to be human should read this novel.

Important: Issues with this Book

This novel was not written for young adults, but it is frequently set for study in high schools, and it is certainly the sort of novel that young adults *should* read, discuss and study. In actual fact, the descriptions of sexual intercourse (including two rapes) and of a violent burglary are by no means as graphic as they might have been.

Disgrace by J.M. Coetzee

Dramatis Personæ – A Selective List of Characters and Historical Figures

Chapters One - Four

David Lurie is a twice-divorced, fifty-two-year-old adjunct Professor of Communications at Cape Technical University in Cape Town, South Africa. His real love is Romantic poetry, of which he teaches only one course. His other time is spent teaching Communications, a discipline he dislikes. As a teacher, he is uninspiring but conscientious. Throughout his life, Lurie has been "a lover of women and, to an extent, a womanizer" (7), but where once women responded automatically to his good looks, he has for some years had to put more effort into seducing them. The year-long arrangement with the prostitute 'Soraya' "has, to his mind, solved the problem of sex rather well" (1). The end of that arrangement is the first of a series of shocks and humiliations that Lurie suffers. As the Wikipedia article puts it, "David Lurie … loses everything: his reputation, his job, his peace of mind, his dreams of artistic success, and finally even his ability to protect his own daughter." The narrative is thus the story of Lurie's education at a time of life when, as he repeatedly says, he is too old to change. But change he does – the world of South Africa leaves him no alternative.

'Soraya' is the professional name of a prostitute David has slept with every Thursday at 2:00 pm for over a year. He met her through *Discreet Escorts* which classifies her as 'exotic' because she is a Muslim. Their relationship ends when, quite by chance, David sees her one Saturday morning shopping in Cape Town with her sons. Shortly after this, 'Soraya' makes the excuse of her mother being ill to suspend their meetings. When David contacts the agency, he is told that she has left; when he phones her (having got her number from a private detective), she denies knowing him and angrily accuses him of harassment. David never sees her again.

'Soraya' is the name of the prostitute supplied by *Discreet Escorts* after the first 'Soraya' stops seeing David. She is "no more than eighteen, unpracticed, to his mind course" (8). He only visits her once.

Dawn is a new secretary in his department. She is married with sons, but is easily seduced by David. In love-making, she "works herself into a froth of excitement that in the end only repels him" (9). They have sex only once, and after that David avoids her.

Melanie Isaacs is a student taking Lurie's Romantics course. She is, "Not the best student but not the worst either: clever enough, but unengaged" (10). Finding her very attractive, Lurie sets out to seduce her and, despite her reluctance, they have sex a number of times. She (perhaps prompted by her boyfriend and/or her father) makes a sexual harassment complaint against him. David never sees her again.

A Study Guide

William Wordsworth (1770-1850) was one of the greatest and most influential of the English Romantic poets.

William Blake (1757-1827) was a poet, painter, and printmaker of the Romantic Period.

Norman McLaren (1914-1987) was an acclaimed Scottish/ Canadian filmmaker.

Rosalind is Lurie's second wife from whom he has been divorced eight years, though they are still on friendly terms. She lives in Cape Town, so they meet up pretty regularly. Rosalind has no illusions about Lurie and is not afraid to tell him his faults and his mistakes.

Ryan is Melanie's boyfriend. He threatens Lurie and vandalizes his car in retaliation for Lurie's affair with Melanie.

Chapters Five – Six

Mr. Isaacs is Melanie's father. He initially asks for Lurie's help to dissuade Melanie from dropping out of university, but when he learns the truth he is outraged by Lurie's conduct.

Elaine Winter is Chair of the Communications department. Lurie feels, "She has never liked him; she regards him as a hangover from the past, the sooner cleared away the better" (38).

Farodia Rassool is a Social Studies professor who is chair of the university-wide committee on discrimination.

Aram Hakim, the Vice-Rector, is a member of Melanie's sexual harassment investigation who tries to save Lurie's job.

Manas Mathabane, Professor of Religious Studies, is the Chair of the Committee of Inquiry into the complaints against Lurie.

Ms van Wyk is the student observer from the Coalition Against Discrimination on the committee.

Chapters Seven – Twelve

Lucy is Lurie's daughter from his first marriage to Evelina who now lives in the Netherlands. Lucy owns a small farm (which Lurie bought for her) in the Eastern Cape where she also runs a boarding kennel. Lucy came to the smallholding as part of a commune six years previously and stayed when the commune broke up. Her partner, Helen, has returned to Johannesburg before Lurie comes to visit after he has been dismissed from his position at the University.

Helen has left the farm months before Lurie's visit. He remembers her as "a large, sad-looking woman with a deep voice and bad skin, older than Lucy. He has never been able to understand what Lucy sees in her; privately he wishes that Lucy would find, or be found by, someone better" (58). Helen does not appear in the narrative.

Disgrace by J.M. Coetzee

Petrus is a black African whom Lucy first describes as "'my new assistant. In fact, since March, my co-proprietor. Quite a fellow'" (60). He has at least two wives and will later suggest that Lucy should also marry him. Petrus is ambition: he wants to own his own land and ultimately to own Lucy's land.

Bev Shaw is a married woman who runs the animal shelter. Lurie initially describes her as "a dumpy, bustling little woman with black freckles, close-cropped hair, and no neck." He is repulsed by the fact that she makes "no effort to be attractive" (70). Later, however, they have an affair.

Bill Shaw is Bev's husband and "equally squat ... with a beet-red face and silver hair.'" Bill greets Lurie as a friend and is always helpful.

Lord Byron (1788-1824) was a major English Romantic poet who was as famous (or infamous) for his scandalous love affairs as for his poetry. Determined to help Greece obtain independence from Turkey, he joined their side in the war in December 1823, but died of fever on April 19, 1824.

Teresa Guiccioli (1800-1873) was the daughter of Count Gamba, a nobleman from Ravenna in Italy. At age seventeen, she was married to the sixty-year-old Count Alessandro Guiccioli as his third wife. She separated from him at the height of her passionate affair with Byron which began in 1819. She was Byron's last mistress whom he left in Italy when he went to Greece. Their relationship is to be the topic of Lurie's opera.

Ettinger is an old Afrikaner neighbor of Lucy's who drives her and Lurie to the hospital following the attack. He is described as "a surly old man who speaks English with a marked German accent" (98). He is a widower whose children have gone back to Germany. Alone, he keeps his home heavily protected against intruders and always carries a gun.

Chapters Thirteen – Twenty-four

Pollux is one of the three South Africans who rape Lucy. (The other two are referred to only as the Tall Man, who seems to be the leader, and the Second Man. Neither reappears after the robbery/rape.) Petrus claims that this youth is his brother-in-law.

Margarita Cogni was the illiterate, twenty-two-year-old wife of a Venetian baker with whom Lord Byron had a short affair in 1817.

Marie Antoinette (1755-1793) was married to the French King Louis XVI. At their palace of Versailles she has a model village built where she could pretend to be a simple shepherdess. She and her husband were executed during the French Revolution.

Evelina was Lurie's first wife. She returned with Lucy to Holland after the divorce and remarried. Lucy, however, did not get on with her step-father and came back to South Africa.

Desiree is Melanie's younger sister. She is even more beautiful than her sister.

Mrs. Isaacs is evidently less than happy with her husband's decision to invite Lurie to dinner.

A Study Guide

Allegra (1817-1822) was Lord Byron's illegitimate daughter by Claire Clairmont (1798-1879), the teenage stepsister of the writer Mary Shelley. Byron, who showed no interest in the child, placed her in a convent where she died at the age of five.

Disgrace by J.M. Coetzee

Genre

Bildungsroman

The genre *Bildungsroman* (the term is of German origin) is a "novel of formation, novel of education, or coming-of-age story ... a literary genre that focuses on the psychological and moral growth of the protagonist from youth to adulthood, and in which, therefore, character change is extremely important" (Wikipedia article). Most novels of this genre end with the protagonist (normally male), wiser in the ways of the world and with greater self-knowledge, moving on to face the further challenges of adulthood. At first glance, this seems to have little to do with a novel about a fifty-two-year-old man. However, in many respects, Lurie is a man who has never grown to maturity. At the start of the novel, he is really still a selfish adolescent, and though he continually protests that he is "too old to heed, too old to change," that is precisely what he does in the course of the novel (204).

Realism

As the name suggests, literary realism aims to represent human experience as it actually is without idealizing or moralizing. Stories in this genre tend to take place in the present or the recent past; are set in places which either actually are or could be real; and concern characters who are involved in plausible incidents and experiences which they deal with in convincing (which often means less than perfect) ways. The issues raised in realistic fiction are ones that a reader could face in his/her life.

Disgrace clearly meets these criteria. Teachers are not infrequently dismissed for having inappropriate sexual relations with their students, and the conflict into which Lurie finds himself thrust in the Eastern Cape is an all too real consequence of the political changes in South Africa in the last few decades – consequences over which none of the characters has any control. Even more fundamentally, the realism of this novel shows itself in the 'messiness' of both characters and their actions. There is so much about the characters that the reader simply never finds out. The reader's uncertainty is nowhere better seen than in the portrayal of the protagonist, David Lurie. For most of the novel, he is a mass of contradictions and as a result acts in ways that surprise and shock the reader who may find them inexplicable. Unlike many novels, there are no clear-cut epiphanies (though there are several epiphanies), no moments of sudden and complete self-knowledge, no definitive point of reformation. Lurie muddles through life. By the end of the novel, he is much more concerned with the feelings of other people (and animals) than he has ever been, but he is far from perfect, and he has no power to change the basic reality in the Eastern Cape.

Narrative voice

Disgrace is written in the third person limited perspective. David Lurie is the protagonist and every character and every event is narrated from his point of view. The Shmoop Editorial Team puts it well:

> The narrator knows David's entire back story, what he's feeling at any given moment, his immediate desires, his worries, and his thoughts. Coetzee often denotes the difference between what the narrator says that David is thinking and what David is really thinking in a given moment by putting David's thoughts in italics. But even then, it doesn't really seem to make a difference – it feels like we're right there in his mind from the get-go. We don't know what any of the other characters are thinking, feeling, or even doing most of the time. ("Narrator Point of View')

The result is that the reader inevitably tends to sympathize with Lurie. Only as the narrative progresses are we increasingly aware that Lurie is not a reliable source; his judgments are slanted by his often inflexible opinions, principles and prejudices.

The novel is narrated in the present tense, which is unusual. The effect is that the reader observes the evolution, regressions and eventual progress of the protagonist at first hand, as it happens, rather than being told about it retrospectively as something that happened in the past. The immediacy of the narrative also accounts for the fact that the narrator reports without judging. The narrator tells us what Lurie is thinking and doing but never tells the reader how these thoughts and actions should be interpreted and evaluated.

Because we see the other characters from the outside, as Lurie does, most of them are pretty confusing leading to a host of unanswered questions: Why does Melanie have sex with Lurie? Why does she come to his apartment and tearfully ask to stay for a while? Was Petrus involved in the attack on Lucy's farm? Why does Bev have sex with Lurie? These and many other questions remain entirely unanswered.

Disgrace by J.M. Coetzee

Setting

The story takes place in post-apartheid South Africa. Apartheid, which in Afrikaans means separateness, was a system of racial segregation introduced by the ruling National Party in 1948 under which the entire population was divided into four racial groups: black, white, colored, and Indian. Black South Africans were deprived of their citizenship and forcibly removed to supposedly self-governing tribal homelands called Bantustans. In 1978, protests around the world and growing opposition at home forced the National Party to begin negotiations with the African National Congress, the leading anti-apartheid political/military movement, with the aim of introducing majority rule. In 1990, Nelson Mandela and other ANC prisoners were released from prison, and in April 1994, the ANC won a parliamentary majority (252 out of 400 seats). On May 10, 1994, Mandela was sworn in as South Africa's first black president.

The action of the novel is not given a date but it can only be two or three years after the end of apartheid. Cape Town, where David is a professor at the University, is still a predominantly white area isolated from the revolutionary changed in the country. Salem, in the Eastern Cape, where the Bantustans were established, is black South Africa, and here the resentment that has built up over decades is tangible. Racial tension is evident in an upsurge of violence perpetrated mainly by young black males seeking revenge against their erstwhile oppressors. The police are overstretched and ineffective. Whites seem to have two choices: wait it out or emigrate.

Themes

Rape

Let's be clear: Melanie and Lucy are *both* raped. The first time he invites her to his flat, Lurie "opens a bottle of Meerlust" (11) (notice the author's play on words there!) and later gives her "a shot of whisky in her coffee" (14). He regards it as part of the seduction ritual. Much later, he will admit to himself that the alcohol "was intended to – the word comes up reluctantly – *lubricate* her" (165). The italics indicate that the word is a euphemism: he was getting her intoxicated to overcome her resistance to the idea of sex. When Melanie avoids him, Lurie "thrusts himself upon her" (22) (note the sexual connotations of the words) and though he desperately needs to believe that it was, "Not rape, not quite that," the reader knows that it was rape because it was "undesired to the core" (23). Seduction rape is still rape.

Lucy is viciously raped by the three black men who rob her house. It is a violent, hate-filled act, at least partly motivated by the decades of resentment caused by apartheid. Thus, although the men are strangers, the act is described by Lucy as "'so personal ... It was done with such personal hatred'" (153).

Melanie does report Lurie's rape of her because she (or her father and/or her boyfriend) are confident that a system exists that will act upon her complaint and they are justified in feeling this because the university calls a committee of inquiry. In contrast, Lucy makes the critical decision not to report the rape because she knows that the police will do nothing to bring the guilty to justice so to her it is a private matter. The rape forever changes Lurie's relationship with his daughter: they are subsequently divided by their gender. Her father is a man and men use their privileged positions, their power, to force themselves on women: that is what the two rapes have in common.

Racial Prejudice

Disgrace is set in a post-apartheid South Africa in which the legacy of centuries of racial hatred and exploitation still haunts the country. Whites, like Lurie, are the inheritors of generation of prejudice and privilege; they instinctively look back nostalgically to the old days when the blacks knew their place. Many disadvantaged blacks, who see the continuing economic disparity between the races, are taking their revenge on their erstwhile oppressors through robbery and rape resulting in a breakdown of law and order that leaves the police virtually helpless.

Few white farmers remain in the Eastern Cape where Lucy lives. Those that do are all heavily armed, but the danger is ever-present and their days are numbered: they will either be murdered or forced out by violence, or they will have their lands transferred to black ownership. Petrus begins as an assistant who helps Lucy around the farm. However, within months, he is no longer in a subservient position having been granted land of his own. It is unclear to what extent Petrus is implicated in the attack on Lucy's farm, but he certainly does protect the youngest of the attackers because he is (Petrus claims) family. Petrus knows that time is running out for the white farmers, and that he only has to wait for his opportunity. Thus, he offers to protect Lucy if she 'marries' him, an arrangement that will effectively give him control of her land. Lucy, pregnant with one of the robbers' children, reluctantly becomes a part of Petrus' extended family. A very clear parallel is implied in the novel between the use that males make of their power over women to abuse them and the use which one race makes of its power to abuse another race (whether this be whites subjugating blacks during apartheid or groups of blacks seeking revenge against isolated whites in post-apartheid South Africa.)

Sex and the Aging Male

At the age of fifty-two, Lurie still has a high sex drive. As a young man he found it very easy indeed to pick up women, "If he looked at a woman in a certain way, with a certain intent, she would return his look, he could rely on that ... Then one day it ended." From that point on, Lurie realized that, "[i]f he wanted a woman he had to learn to pursue her; often, in one way or another, to buy her" (7). For the last year, he has "solved the problem of sex" (1) by weekly meetings with a prostitute ('Soraya') where he achieves what he calls "a moderate bliss, a moderated bliss" (5). When this arrangement is shattered by his own intrusion into the woman's private life, he has two unsatisfactory sexual encounters. The replacement 'Soraya' he finds "unpractised, to his mind coarse" (8) and Dawn, with whom sex is "a failure" because "[b]ucking and clawing, she works herself into a froth of excitement that in the end only repels him" (9). It is clear to the reader (if not to Lurie) that he wants something more than moderate physical pleasure from his sexual encounters.

Then he sees Melanie and feels a rush of desire. Aware that it might be the last great passion he will ever feel, he makes no effort to resist it, as he might have done in the past. In having an affair with a student, Lurie crosses departmental, generational and ethical boundaries. [In pursuing his own desires (the same impulses celebrated by the Romantic poets whom he loves) he abuses his position of power.] He ignores Melanie's reluctance to have sex and on one occasion effectively rapes her. In the new climate of sexual awareness (Lurie says that they are living in "'puritanical times'" [64]), what he has done is condemned and the university demands a public statement of contrition which Lurie refuses to give. He may genuinely feel that he has been "enriched" by his affair with Melanie (53), and with the other women he has had in his life, but as his daughter points out, he should not assume that the same was true of his partners. In the same vein, his former wife Rosalind tells him, "'[Y]ou were always a great self-deceiver, David'" (184).

When he has sex with Bev Shaw, a married woman whom he finds physically unattractive, he reflects, "After the sweet young flesh of Melanie

Isaacs, this is what I have come to. This is what I have to get used to. This and even less than this." He falls into self pity over the way in which age has robbed him of his attractiveness, telling himself to "stop calling her poor Bev Shaw. If she is poor, he is bankrupt" (147). Yet there is a more positive aspect to his affair with Bev. She is, after all, more his age, the sex they have is consensual, and sex soon gives way to simple tenderness. Lurie's perception of his own aging is also evident in the changing nature of his Byron opera when he decides to shift his focus from Teresa as a young woman to when she is middle-aged and past passion, as he now realizes that he himself is past passion.

Fathers and Daughters

David Lurie desperately wants to be a good father – perhaps he wants it too much. The problem is that, until right at the end of the novel, Lurie wants to control his daughter's life. One of the hardest lessons he has to learn in the course of the narrative is that he behaves as though everything his daughter does is part of the story of his life. Lucy tells him, "'You are the main character, I am a minor character'" (193). By the conclusion of the novel, Lurie has learned that his role as father is to support Lucy in the decisions she has taken about the life she wants to live. He has also understood that he will be a grandfather. There is a great leap in self knowledge in his admission, "As a father he had not been much of a success, despite trying harder than most. As a grandfather he will probably score lower than average too" (212).

Disgrace

Both Lurie and Lucy have to suffer the stigma of disgrace, Lurie because of his sexual misconduct with a student, and Lucy because she has been raped and will bear an illegitimate child. Their reaction is, however, very different. Lurie is angry about his treatment by the university and outraged by the rape of his daughter and the inability of the police to bring the culprits to justice. (The reader, but not Lurie, appreciates the irony that he, who was judged and punished for his rape of Melanie, is now seeking justice on behalf of Lucy for the rape that she suffered.) Lucy is traumatized by the rape, and by the fact that, in order to keep her land, she has to agree to Petrus' proposal of 'marriage'. Both father and daughter agree that the destruction of their high hopes is humiliating, but Lucy says this:

> "Yes, I agree, it is humiliating. But perhaps that is a good place to start from again. Perhaps that is what I must learn to accept. To start at ground level. With nothing. Not with nothing but. With nothing. No cards, no weapons, no property, no rights, no dignity." (200)

That is what Lucy learns herself and what she teaches Lurie.

Disgrace by J.M. Coetzee

Animal and Humans

David applies absolute standards. In this, he is a true Romantic. It is this tendency to believe in timeless principles (such as the purity of desire and the right to remain silent) that gets him into so much trouble before the committee of inquiry and that leads him uncompromisingly to demand justice for his daughter. He is simply not prepared to compromise. During a heated discussion about the life she has chosen to live, Lucy tells her father, "'there is no higher life. This is the only life there is. Which we share with the animals.'" This goes against Lurie's belief in absolute principles. He agrees that "'this is the only life there is,'" but objects to equating human and animal life. He tells his daughter:

> As for the animals, by all means let us be kind to them. But let us not lose perspective. We are of a different order of creation from the animals. Not higher necessarily, just different. So if we are going to be kind, let it be out of simple generosity, not because we feel guilty or fear retribution. (72)

Ironically, given this unpromising starting point, animals play a key role in Lurie's development. Initially, he denies that animals have souls and has an instinctive dislike of people like Bev who support Animal Welfare. Almost immediately, however, he begins to form relationships with animals. First, there is Katy, the abandoned dog in Lucy's kennels with whom he feels a certain empathy given that he has just lost his job. Second, he sees and assists Bev in treating and euthanizing sick animals and gains a new respect for her. Eventually, Lurie finds his purpose in disposing of the bodies of dead dogs in a respectful way. In these ways, the egocentric protagonist learns to show increased concern for those other than himself. Finally, he has to learn that there is no distinction between animal and human life, which means that he must abandon his absolutism (i.e. his tendency to see everything as a matter of principle) and learn how to compromise in order to survive.

It is not difficult to see a parallel between Lurie's initial attitude to animals and the attitudes of the whites to the black population of South Africa. Lurie is not overtly racist, but he has lived a sheltered life in Cape Town and when he moves to the Eastern Cape he has his first close contact with ordinary black South Africans. Lurie's initial reaction is reactionary. We are told, "Phrases that all his life he has avoided seem suddenly just and right: *Teach him a lesson. Show him his place.*" However, almost immediately, Lurie is self-critical, "So this is what it is like, he thinks! This is what it is like to be a savage!" (200). Finally he has to learn that the apartheid distinctions between white and black no longer exist, which means that he must abandon his racial absolutism and learn how to compromise in order to survive.

Symbolism

The Byron Opera

The story of Byron's love affairs in Italy and of his subsequent death at age thirty-six in Greece provides a parallel narrative to Lurie's own story since Byron left England for Italy because his love affairs had become a scandal; that is, because he has become a disgrace. There is no doubt that in the early part of the novel Lurie identifies himself with Byron, the slightly older man with the beautiful young mistress (he over thirty, Teresa Guiccoli only nineteen). There is a great deal of wishful thinking in such an identification, not least because, while Teresa seems to have been passionately in love with Byron, Melanie appears almost indifferent to Lurie. More than the historical story itself, however, Lurie's evolving attempts to write an opera *Byron in Italy* provides a guide to his changing attitudes to love, to sex and to himself. We are told that he originally conceived the opera "as a chamber-play about love and death, with a passionate young woman and a once-passionate but now less than passionate older man." Like Lurie in the Eastern Cape, Byron "has begun to long for quiet retirement; failing that, for apotheosis, for death" (176). Significantly, Lurie can write dialogue for Byron but not for Teresa. This might be taken to indicate his inability to see his affair with Melanie from the young woman's viewpoint.

Following his return to Cape Town, Lurie decides to write the libretto from the point of view of the middle-aged Teresa who is "a dumpy little widow" left only with the memories of the dead Byron, the one passion of her life:

> The passage of time has not treated Teresa kindly. With her heavy bust, her stocky trunk, her abbreviated legs, she looks more like a peasant, a *contadina*, than an aristocrat. The complexion that Byron once so admired has turned hectic; in summer she is overtaken with attacks of asthma that leave her heaving for breath.

Lurie now identifies himself with Teresa rather than Byron; her fate does engage "his heart as his heart is now" (177). Like Teresa, he needs desperately to believe that his former passionate affairs (and particularly his last great passion for Melanie) constituted the apex of his life, the one thing that set him apart from other men. Yet for Teresa there is no validation, for the ghost of Byron replies 'derisively: *Leave me, leave me, leave me be!*" (181). Effectively, Melanie is saying the same to him – though rather more brutally.

Like the middle-aged Teresa, Lurie could howl "to the moon for the rest of her natural life in a fever that set him howling too," except that another character "emerges from the dark." It is Allegra, the illegitimate daughter whom Byron largely ignored and who is now dying of malaria. Allegra is also calling for her father who can only lament his shabby treatment of her because he is dead. Without actually articulating it, Lurie must see the parallel between his own daughter's need of him – the main difference being that, unlike Byron, he is *not* yet dead. He has, however, been neglecting her because he has concentrated entirely on his own passions. The opera in its final form is a call to action in the real world, and appropriately Lurie will acknowledge that it will never be finished, never be performed. He will no longer strive to act through literature but through practical action to do what little he can to improve the lives of humans and animals alike.

A Study Guide

Study Guide: Translations, Questions and Commentary

This novel deserves to be read *reflectively*. The notes aim to give necessary background information. The questions are *not* designed to test you but to help you to locate and to understand characters, plot, settings, issues, and themes in the text. They do not normally have simple answers, nor is there always one answer. Consider a range of possible interpretations - preferably by *discussing* the questions with others. Disagreement is to be encouraged! The commentary explores the text in depth.

Chapter One

Translations

"*luxe e volupté*" (1) – luxury and voluptuousness.
"*Oedipus*" (2) – *Oedipus Rex* (*Oedipus Tyrannus* or *Oedipus the King*) by Sophocles (c.429 BC) is a play in which the tragic protagonist discovers that he has unknowingly murdered his own father and married, and had children by, his own mother. Oedipus blinds himself as punishment for his crimes.
"*la donna è mobile*" (3) – the woman is adaptable/ fickle.
"*nom de commerce*" (8) – trade name.

Questions

1. In the course of the chapter, Lurie refers to a number of disappointments and failures in his life. As you read, make a note of each of them.

2. Lurie describes the sex he has with Soraya as "rather like the copulation of snakes: lengthy, absorbed, but rather abstract, rather dry, even at its hottest" (2). Contrast this with the sex he has (once) with Soraya's replacement and (once) with Dawn. Why does he find the former "bliss … a moderate bliss, a moderated bliss" (5), but the sex with the second Soraya "coarse" (8) and that with Dawn "a failure" (9). What is he ideally looking for in his sexual relations?

3. Explain why Lurie's seemingly ideal arrangement with Soraya ends. What does this tell us about Lurie's limitations as a person?

Commentary

David Lurie is convinced that Elaine Winter, the chair of the Communications Department in which he teaches at Cape Technical University, "regards him as a hangover from the past" (38). Whether or not Winter actually holds this view, it is an accurate picture of Lurie. Originally a Professor of Classics and Modern Languages at Cape Town University College, he has seen the university change its name and his department closed down "as part of the great rationalization." Now he teaches Communications 101, a discipline whose "first premise" he finds "preposterous" (3); his academic

Disgrace by J.M. Coetzee

passion is for the Romantic poets. Lurie is out of tune with the modern academic world and (as we shall see later) with the changes in South Africa since the end of apartheid.

"For a man of his age, fifty-two, divorced, he has, to his mind, solved the problem of sex rather well" (1). It is interesting that he uses the word "problem" in relation to sex. Presumably he means that sex is a physical need that he wants to satisfy without the messy attachments that come with a relationship, for as he has got older he has lost the ability instantly to attract women and has had to learn to pursue them. The solution is an arrangement without complications and emotional ties: he employs Soraya through *Discreet Escorts* to have sex with him on Thursdays afternoons. Lurie is happy to think of himself as a man who "lives within his income, within his temperament, within his emotional means" (2).

Although Lurie tries to maintain a discreet separation between the physical act with Soraya and his awareness of her as a person, certain aspects of Soraya interest him on a human level: the fact that *Discreet Escorts* takes half of the money he pays her, which seems excessive; the contradiction between her occupation and her prudish attitude to nude beaches and her unsympathetic attitude to beggars; and the fact that she is a Muslim. He is tempted to ask her to have sex with him outside the confines of Windsor Mansions, to spend the night with him, but he does not suggest it because it would turn their understanding into a relationship.

However, Lurie has convinced himself that there is more between Soraya and himself than a simple financial arrangement, "an affection has grown up in him for her. To some degree, he believes, this affection is returned" (1-2). This is the first example of Lurie's capacity for self-deception: on one level, he knows that he is simply buying Soraya, but on another he is convinced that "at the level of temperament her affinity with him can surely not be feigned" (3). This romanticized self-deception is shattered when they see each other by chance in Cape Town where she is shopping with her two children. Lurie's immediate reaction is that the incident brings him closer to Soraya, "he feels, if anything, greater tenderness for her. *Your secret is safe with me*, he would like to say (6), but he soon notices that her attitude to him has changed, "Though Soraya still keeps her appointments, he feels a growing coolness as she transforms herself into just another woman and him into just another client." (7) Soraya soon breaks off the arrangement, and when Lurie, desperate to find her, calls her on the phone, Soraya denies that she knows him and accuses him of harassment. Reality hits Lurie hard, "Her shrillness surprises him: there has been no intimation of it before" (9). [Look out for Lurie being told a similarly brutal truth about Melanie's feelings about him near the end of the book.]

The theme of the changes in South Africa is introduced through the character of Dawn who, with her family, is waiting to emigrate to New Zealand because of the rising crime rate and the impotence of the police. She comments on how conditions have changed for people of Lurie's generation, "'I mean, whatever the rights and wrongs of the situation, at least you knew where you were … Now people just pick and choose which laws they want to obey. It's anarchy'" (8). This is a reality from which Lurie has been sheltered by his position, but one with which he will have to come to terms in the course of the novel.

Disgrace by J.M. Coetzee

Chapter Two

Questions

4. Lurie meets Melanie in "the old college gardens" (10). Remembering the reference to snakes in Chapter One, comment on the significance of this detail.
5. Explain why Melanie rejects Lurie's sexual advances. Do you think that she will subsequently sleep with him? Explain your answer.

Commentary

Separated from Soraya, and having failed to find satisfaction with her replacement or with Dawn, "the problem of sex" (1) reemerges. He meets Melanie Isaacs, a student in his Romantics class, by chance in the college garden on his way home one afternoon and sets out to seduce her. When he first takes her to his flat, he thinks, "the girl he has brought home is not just thirty years his junior: she is a student, his student, under his tutelage" (11). This should ring alarm bells about what it is that he is planning to do, but it does not.

As in his relationship with Soraya, Lurie deceives himself about what is happening. On one level he knows that his advances are inappropriate and unwelcome: he is thirty years older than Melanie, and she does not even share his interests for the Norman McLaren movie or for Wordsworth. He knows also that he is going through a ritual of seduction (which includes plying the woman with alcohol to lower her defenses), but he has to make it seem something more than this. He "wills the girl to be captivated" by the dance movie. He justifies her having sex with him in romantic terms telling her, "'a woman's beauty does not belong to her alone. It is part of the bounty she brings into the world. She has a duty to share it.'" While he knows that these words are simply a seduction line, "at this moment he believes in them" (15). For Lurie their sex (if it happens) must be more than merely physical appetite.

Similarly, he cannot bear to think of himself as a seducer, so from the start he projects desire on Melanie, "Does she know he has an eye on her? Probably. Women are sensitive to it, to the weight of the desiring gaze" (10). He notes her "coquettish little smile" (11) because he must make her complicit in what may happen between them. The reader is never given any insight into Melanie's actual feelings: we see her through Lurie's eyes, but this does not mean that the reader simply accepts his viewpoint.

Again, as with Soraya, there are hints that Melanie has a life of which he knows nothing. She asks, "'And what if I already share it [i.e., her beauty]?'" (15). Lurie fails to register the implication that Melanie already has a boyfriend. This is a reality that he will eventually have to confront.

Chapter Three

Translation

"*Kaaps*" (21) – An accent local to the Cape area.

Questions

6. How does the pattern of detachment followed by personal involvement that Lurie has experienced with Soraya repeat itself in his relationship with Melanie?

7. At the end of the chapter, Lurie reflects, "She is behaving badly, getting away with too much; she is learning to exploit him and will probably exploit him further" (26). Do you think that Lurie's suspicions are justified? Why do you think that Melanie asks to stay with him for a while?

Commentary

In Lurie, reality continues to battle with desire and desire with his need to see what is happening as something more noble than mere lust. Lurie admits that this "is where he ought to end it. But he does not." Instead, he accesses Melanie's file (a clear misuse of his position) and invites her to lunch. He immediately notices that "her hips are as slim as a twelve-year-old's," which again should be a warning but is not (11). She admits that she may be worried about their relationship, but he tells her, "'No need. I'll take care. I won't let it go too far'" (17). His confidence that he can control the situation is self-delusion for the chapter makes it clear that Lurie is "in the grip of something. Beauty's rose..." that he cannot control (16).

Finally, Lurie seduces Melanie. She is "passive throughout" their lovemaking which he finds "so pleasurable that from its climax he tumbles into blank oblivion." When they part, Lurie notes that, "Averting her face, she frees herself [from him]" (17). The wording here implies that he knows that he has in some sense forced her against her will. After that one encounter, Melanie avoids him and, when she cannot do that evades his attempt to repeat having sex. When he picks her up in his car, reality intrudes when he realizes that she is, "*A child! No more than a child!*" and asks himself "*What am I doing?*" Yet, he is not in control because, "his heart lurches with desire" (18).

In his lecture, Lurie tells the class that Wordsworth is trying to find a balance between the purity of his "'living thought'" and reality which presents itself as "'a soulless image, a mere image on the retina'" (19). This is directly relevant to Lurie who is always rejecting matter-of-fact reality for an abstract conception which makes what he is doing appear more noble, more significant than it is. In his sexual life, Lurie is trying to find a balance between the purely physical and the inevitable involvement in the whole relationship. His problem is that the girl who had been "just another pretty face in class" has become "a

Disgrace by J.M. Coetzee

presence in his life, a breathing presence" as had Soraya (21). He is repeating the mistake he made with her.

Not taking the hint of Melanie's avoidance of him, Lurie begins to stalk her. He would not see going to watch her rehearse in those terms, but he comes close telling himself, "He ought to be gone ... [It is an] unseemly business, sitting in the dark spying on a girl (unbidden the word *letching* comes to him)." He forces himself on her at her cousin's house. He notices, but is not deterred by, her passivity, "She does not resist. All she does is avert herself: avert her lips, avert her eyes" (22). He is desperate to assure himself that what he does is, "Not rape, not quite that" (a conclusion with which the reader might not agree), but he is honest enough to admit that on Melanie's part it is "undesired nevertheless, undesired to the core." He realizes that it has been, "A mistake, a huge mistake," and imagines Melanie taking a bath, trying to purify "cleanse herself" of having been with him (23). It seems that at this moment Lurie's Wordsworthian attempt to balance "the sense image" with "the idea that lies buried more deeply in the soil of memory" has failed (20). Objective reality has shattered his Romantic illusions.

Lurie began to pursue Melanie out of pure selfishness: his intention was that his "quick little affair" with Melanie would be "quickly in quickly out" (the author's rather brutal pun on the sex act), is destroyed when Melanie asks (without any explanation) to stay with him for a while. He thinks, "Now she is in his house, trailing complications behind her" (24). He had been seeking, "A last leap of the flame of sense before it goes out" (25), but has got himself involved in a relationship with real dangers for his career (remember he has falsified his class records for her). He, the pursuer, is trapped, though he is honest enough to admit that "if she has got away with much, he has got away with more; if she is behaving badly, he has behaved worse ... Let him not forget that" (26).

The theme of "the new South Africa" is again touched on in the play *Sunset at the Globe Salon* in which, "Catharsis seems to be the presiding principle: all the coarse old prejudices brought into the light of day and washed away in gales of laughter" (21). This is Lurie's cynical verdict on truth and reconciliation. The change in South Africa will prove to be another and more fundamental reality that Lurie will be forced to acknowledge.

Chapter Four

Translation

"*coup de main*" (29) – sudden, surprise attack.

Questions

8. Lurie denies that he is 'collecting' Melanie. Do you agree with his own assessment of his conduct toward her?
9. In what ways is Lurie like the Lucifer of Byron's poem *Lara*?

Commentary

Lurie and Melanie have sex "one more time" which foreshadows the end of their relationship. This occurs in his daughter's bed which raised for the reader implications of incest. Once again, he projects into Melanie the sort of sexual response he needs to believe her to have, "She is quick and greedy for experience. If he does not sense in her a fully sexual appetite, that is only because she is so young" (27). This explanation, of course, absolves him of all guilt; it makes him her guide and teacher.

Suddenly, Lurie begins to face consequences for the way he has acted. He reflects, "the chickens come home to roost. I should have guessed it, a girl like that would not come unencumbered." A young man, presumably Melanie's boyfriend, comes into his office that afternoon and warns him not to "'think you can just walk into people's lives and walk out again when it suits you'" (28); his car is vandalized; and on Monday, when Melanie reappears in class, she is accompanied by her boyfriend. When Laurie asks the class about Lucifer, the boyfriend, obviously aiming his comment at Lurie says, "'He does what he feels like. He doesn't care if it's good or bad. He just does it'" (31).

Throughout the chapter, Lurie patronizes Melanie, "Despite himself, his heart goes out to her. Poor little bird, he thinks, whom I have held against my breast" (29), and later, "Again his heart goes out to her. If they were alone he would embrace her, try to cheer her up. *My little dove*, he would call her" (32). This is dangerous self-deception for it ignores the fact that he has given Melanie the power to destroy him; it ignores the fact that he does not really know her. His stereotyping reduces her humanity.

When Lurie talks to Melanie in his office, he hypocritically talks of his "'obligations to my students.'" He tells her that she will have to attend class more regularly and make up a missed test – in, fact, he attempts to wipe out what has happened between them and re-establish their former teacher-student relationship. (This will later link with his resentment at the changes in South Africa since the end of apartheid and his longing to the days when the whites were the unquestioned masters.) Looking at her, however, Lurie sees that Melanie will not let this happen. She seems to want to tell him, "*You have cut me off from everyone ... You have made me bear your secret. I am no longer just your student. How can you speak to me like this?"* (32). This foreshadows that things are not going to end well for Lurie.

Although he does not know it, his final sight of Melanie is riding on the back of her boyfriend's motorcycle. She "sits with knees wide apart, pelvis arched. A quick shudder of lust tugs him. *I have been there!* He thinks" (33). For a moment, Lurie allows his romantic idealization of their relationship to give way to the reality that it has been no more than the desire of a predator collecting another lover – something that earlier he had assured Melanie that he was not doing.

Chapter Five

Translation
"*Schadenfreude*" (40) – a German word meaning a feeling of enjoyment that comes from seeing or hearing about the troubles of other people.

Questions
10. The section following the confrontation with Mr. Isaacs opens, "This is how it begins" (36). What mood does this sentence set?
11. Explain the final paragraph of the chapter.

Commentary
Lurie's class on Byron's poem "Lara" has foreshadowed his own fall from grace. In it, Melanie's boyfriend identified him with Lucifer, the being who, "'does what he feels like. He doesn't care if it's good or bad. He just does it'" (31). When he is first contacted by Melanie's father, Lurie puts him off with "lies and evasions," but he acknowledges to himself that he is guilty, "*I am the worm in the apple*" – an oblique reference to the temptation of Eve by Satan (35). When Mr. Isaac's confronts Lurie having discovered the truth, he tells him, "We put our children in the hands of you people because we think we can trust you ... We never thought we were sending our daughter into a nest of vipers" (36). This is a reference (conscious, one assumes, since Isaacs is later shown to be very religious) to Matthew 23:33, "Ye serpents, ye generation of vipers, how can ye escape the damnation of hell?" (KJV). This again identified Lurie with Lucifer.

In conversation with his ex-wife Rosalind, Lurie hears a very different account of his affair with Melanie. Rosalind reminds him of the reality of his age and asks rhetorically, "'Do you think a young girl finds any pleasure with a man of that age [i.e. 52]?'"(41). Of course, this is precisely what the reader has seen Lurie convincing himself of. (See page 26.) Rosalind adds, "'You are too old to be meddling with other people's children ... The whole thing is disgraceful from beginning to end. Disgraceful and vulgar too'" (43). This is, indeed, harsh reality smashing down Lurie's romantic idealization. Only when he realizes the disgrace of his earlier life will Lurie be able to move on, but that will take honesty.

Consequences quickly follow. The following day: he is informed that a sexual harassment complaint has been filed against him, and he is called to a meeting in the office of Aram Hakim (the Vice-Rector), that is also attended by his department chair, Elaine Winter, and the university chair, Farodia Rassool. Only two students attend for his class on Baudelaire, which he explains as the result of gossip about his 'disgrace', though it might equally represent a lack of interest on the part of students. The lawyer Lurie consults tells him to take a purely pragmatic view of the charges, "'You give certain undertakings perhaps take a spell of leave, in return for which the university persuades the girl, or her family, to drop the charges'" (40). However, Lurie reacts negatively to this advice: he is offended by the notion of having counseling to "cure" him. His attitude foreshadows that he will prove inflexible. The following morning the local newspaper carries a sensationalized story with the headline "'Professor on sex charge'" (43).

Chapter Six

Questions

12. Describe the attitude that Lurie, from the very start, adopts before the academic committee investigating the charges of harassment brought against him.
13. Explain why it is important to Lurie to describe and understand the hearing as a trial rather than as an inquiry.
14. Lurie clearly does not feel sorry for his conduct toward Melanie. Why exactly is that?

Commentary

Throughout the committee hearing, Lurie argues with the Chairman about whether or not what they are holding is a trial. Lurie wants to treat it as a trial because then he can plead guilty to both charges and, as he tells the committee, that will "'let us get on with our lives'" (46). Lurie refuses every effort by the Chairman to couch the hearing in language other than that of a trial because he senses that the members are seeking much more than a guilty plea: they want a confession and a statement of contrition. The former he will reluctantly give them, but the latter he will not because he does not feel sorry for what he did with Melanie. He tells one of the members that he will not open his mind to the committee:

> What goes on in my mind is my business, not yours, Farodia. Frankly, what you want from me is not a response but a confession. Well, I make no confession. I put forward a plea. As is my right. Guilty as charged. That is my plea. That is as far as I am willing to go. (48-49)

In fact, he does go further in response to their insistence. He says, "'You want a confession, I give you a confession. As for the impulse, it is far from ungovernable. I have denied similar impulses many times in the past, I am ashamed to say'" (50). Here Lurie's defense is based on the holiness of impulse, desire and passion – an attitude central to Romantic poetry. When he actually says, "'I took advantage of my position vis-à-vis Ms Isaacs. It was wrong, and I regret it'" (52), this is still not enough because the committee wants to know that he means it. This causes Lurie to withdraw his confession and he adopts a defiant tone when a student reporter asks if he regrets what he did. Lurie replies, "'No ... I was enriched by the experience'" (53).

The Chairman of the committee points out that if he makes a full statement admitting he was wrong to do what he did and acknowledging that he is willing to accept recommendations that the committee makes, he might be able to save his job and his pension. Lurie refuses. What he is refusing to do is to admit that acting upon his sexual desires was wrong because the woman, although twenty years of age, was his student at the time; he is denying that he was guilty of "mixing power relations with sexual relations" (50). To the committee, Lurie is guilty of "'abuse,'" and it is that word which appears twice in the statement he is eventually asked to sign. (See page 55.) This statement has "'the status of a plea in mitigation, [and] the Rector will be prepared to accept it in ... [a] spirit of repentance'" (55). Lurie refuses because, he says, "'Repentance belongs to another world, to another universe of discourse'" (57). When the Chairman tells Lurie that all that is required is a public statement, and that members of the university cannot know if he has repented in his soul, Lurie calls out the obvious hypocrisy.

All of this puts the reader in a difficult position. Because the narrative presents everything from Lurie's viewpoint, we tend to sympathize with him (rather as we do with Meursault in Albert Camus' *The Stranger* and with Joseph K. in Franz Kafka's *The Trial*). The machinations of the committee do indeed seem hypocritical: all they want is for Lurie to jump through certain moral hoops and then the university will normalize the situation – perhaps even let him return to teaching. It is a public relations exercise. Lurie, by contrast, is being true to what he feels: he will not say he is sorry for something for which he is not sorry, even to keep his job. On the other hand, Lurie clearly acted inappropriately and selfishly in his manipulation of Melanie: he is a rapist who *should* be ashamed. That he is not shows that he puts himself above the moral laws of society. More importantly, it shows how out of touch he is with the new climate of sexual relations. Just as he has not come to terms with a multi-racial South Africa, Lurie has not understood that men can no longer use their power to dominate and abuse women. Lurie is living in the past, both in the age of the Romantics and in the age of apartheid.

It has been suggested that Lurie's hearing before the committee of inquiry is an allegory of the Truth and Reconciliation Committee that was formed in South Africa by the *Promotion of National Unity and Reconciliation Act* in 1995 (Sherrod, *Gradesaver*, Chapters 5 and 6). On this reading, Lurie's use of his status and gender to have sex with Melanie parallels the suppression by white supremacists of black South Africans during apartheid. Most witnesses came forward and publically confessed their part in committing atrocities, and those who did so were given amnesty. In this light, Lurie's adamant refusal to express regret for his action looks even less acceptable.

A Study Guide

Chapter Seven

Translations

"*boervrou*" (58) – an Afrikaans term for a peasant woman.

"*kombi*" (62) – a vehicle like a small bus that can carry about ten people.

"*Qu'est devenu ce front poli, ces cheveux blonds, sour-cils voûtés?*" (63) – What became of that polished forehead, that blond hair, arched eyebrows?

Questions

15. Explain the ominous foreboding in this chapter. Make a list of examples of foreshadowing.

16. What attitude does Lucy take to her father's seduction of a student? What attitude does she take to his defiant attitude toward the university?

Commentary

The fact that Lucy uses her father's first name, David, shows how far she is from accepting him as a father. Lucy willingly offers her father "'refuge on an indefinite basis'" (63). When he first sees his daughter, Lurie notes that she is putting on weight. He sees her as "a throwback, this sturdy young settler" to the original white pioneers who settled and farmed the land (58). He is aware of the dangers of a white women being so isolated, but still he is looking back into history not forward.

Lucy is realistic and non-judgmental about his seduction of a student, since, as she tells Lurie, "'It must go on all the time. It certainly did when I was a student. If they prosecuted every case the profession would be decimated.'" Lucy is less tolerant of her father's inflexible attitude to the university's demands, even when he explains that re-education, reformation and counseling reminds him "'too much of Mao's China. Recantation, self-criticism, public apology. I'm old fashioned, I would prefer simply to be put up against a wall and shot. Have done with it.'" Lurie complains about the "'puritanical times'" in which they live. This again places him as a man stuck in the past, as unaware of the progress of women's rights movements as he is of the movements for black equality. Lucy tells him, "'You shouldn't be so unbending, David. It isn't heroic to be unbending'" (64). This conversation establishes the key difference between father and daughter: the father is principled and living in a by-gone era when principles meant something, and the daughter is practical, pragmatic and adaptive in a South Africa that is changing very quickly, and not always for the better.

Lurie is also backward-looking in his attitude to his affair with Melanie. We learn:

> Without warning a memory of the girl comes back: of her neat little breasts with their upstanding nipples, of her smooth flat belly. A ripple of desire passes

through him. Evidently whatever it was is not over yet. (62-63)

This is entirely unrealistic since it does not take into consideration the feelings of Melanie, for whom evidently it *is* all over.

Chapter Eight

Translation

"duiker" (71) – a small antelope found in Southern Africa.

Question

17. Explain Lurie's prejudice against "'animal welfare people'" (71).

Commentary

Lurie talks with Lucy about his affair with Melanie. He continues to defend her, blaming others for the complaint against him, and he continues to defend his own conduct in terms of being true to his desires. He asks Lucy, "'Do you remember Blake? ... 'Sooner murder an infant in its cradle than nurse unacted desires'? ... Unacted desires turn as ugly in the old as in the young'" (67). He speaks of his affairs idealistically, "'Every woman I have been close to has taught me something about myself. To that extent they have made me a better person.'" Lucy jokingly suggests that they might not say the same about their relationship with him. In contrast to her father, Lucy is a pragmatist. When he asks if she is living the life she wants, Lucy replies, "'It will do'" (68). Later Lucy confronts him with being dissatisfied with the life she has made for herself. She admits that her friends "'are not going to lead me to a higher life, and the reason is, there is no higher life. There is only the life there is.'" The difference between father and daughter is that while she sees herself living the same life as the animals do, Lurie insists that "'We are a different order of creating from animals. Not higher, necessarily, just different'" (72). This entirely different view of life will lead to friction and misunderstanding later on. It is partly a gender gap because, as Lucy tells him, "'Women can be surprisingly forgiving'" (67)

The country is a very different kind of life from the one he has lived in Cape Town, and this brings home to Lurie the serious consequences of his action. He reflects:

> Two weeks ago he was in a classroom explaining to the bored youth of the country the distinction between drink and drink up, burned and burnt. The perfective, signifying an action carried through to its conclusion. How far away it all seems! I live, I have lived, I lived. (69)

His affair with Melanie exemplified the perfect tense ("an action carried through to its conclusion"). That is what makes him so inflexible.

Lucy's world is immediately uncomfortable to Lurie. He has already noticed that his daughter has put on weight and that none of her friends is attractive. This is particularly true of Bev Shaw because, "He does not like women who make no effort to be attractive. It is a resistance he has had to

Disgrace by J.M. Coetzee

Lucy's friends before. Nothing to be proud of: a prejudice that has settled in his mind, settled down" (70). Another element of prejudice is his negative reaction to those who care for animals because he has always regarded humans as inherently superior (he says "different") to animals. Again, his reaction to Bev Shaw epitomizes his feelings:

> He has nothing against animal lovers with whom Lucy has been mixed up as long as he can remember. The world would no doubt be a worse place without them. So when Bev Shaw opens her front door he puts on a good face, though in fact he is repelled by the odours of cat urine and dog mange and Jeyes Fluid that greets them. (70)

Lurie has a lot to learn.

Chapter Nine

Questions

18. What leads Lurie to sat to Lucy, "'It's not working out, is it? Shall I leave?'" (73)? What is her reaction?

19. What prompts Lurie to ask for Lucy's forgiveness at the end of the chapter?

Commentary

Lucy makes various suggestions to help her father adjust to rural life. He agrees to help Petrus in establishing his land saying, "'I like the historical piquancy'" referring to the reversal of roles from the founding of the country when black people were used as labor by white farmers (74). Things are changing in South Africa. Lucy tells Lurie that Petrus is now "'a man of substance. Ask him to pay you [for your labor]. He can afford it. I'm not sure I can afford him anymore'" (75). In just a few months, the relationship between Lucy and her 'assistant' has changed radically, though she seems able to adapt to it.

Lurie also agrees to help Bev Shaw, though he insists:

> "It sounds suspiciously like community service. It sounds like someone trying to make reparation for past misdeeds ... I'll do it. But only as long as I don't have to become a better person. I am not prepared to be reformed. I want to go on being myself." (75)

Although Lurie is not being totally serious, the reader sees again his inflexibility, an inflexibility which will make it hard for him to adapt to the changes that are happening on his daughter's own farm. Lucy replies in down-to-earth fashion that the animals will not care about his motives. Ironically, his exposure to the love and care that Bev gives to animals will awaken in Lurie and understanding of unselfish love for others; it will be part of the process by which he becomes a better person.

Lurie grows attached to an abandoned bulldog named Katy who is depressed and unresponsive. In her, he finds commonality, "'Abandoned, are we?'" (76). He feels enough of a connection to the dog to fall asleep in her cage. At the end of the chapter, he does something remarkable: he asks Lucy to forgive him. When she asks why, he explains, "'For being one of the two mortals assigned to usher you into the world and for not turning out to be a better guide'" (77). This new humility and willingness to admit error is surprising to the reader since Lurie has previously come across as arrogant and self-righteous.

We notice that once again Lurie feels "a light shudder of voluptuousness" at the thought of Melanie (75). He just can't seem to shake his attachment to her – an attachment that exists only on his side and is therefore unrealistic.

Disgrace by J.M. Coetzee

Chapter Ten

Translations

"*boytjie!*" (79) – South African slang for a jock (an athletic older man).
"*tessitura*" (79) – weaving of hairs.
"Faro" (85) – a betting card game.

Questions

20. Lurie reflects on Bev Shaw, "Lucy thought he would find her interesting. But Lucy is wrong. Interesting is not the word" (83). What do you think is the word? Explain.

21. How does Lurie feel about Lucy's lesbianism?

Commentary

When Lurie goes to the animal clinic, his first impression is once again how unattractive Bev is. He describes her features and concludes, "'As an ensemble, remarkably unattractive'" (79). This superficial judgment is, however, challenged when he observes and assists her in helping sick animals. He reflects:

> Things are beginning to fall into place. He has a first inkling of the task this ugly little woman has set herself ... Bev Shaw, not a veterinarian but a priestess ... Lucy thought he would find her interesting. But Lucy is wrong. Interesting is not the word. (83)

He is fascinated by her role as a powerful force in the community, and is also impressed by Bev's attitude to his reason for being there. Bev knows only that he is "'just in trouble'" and wants to know no more. Her acceptance draws from Lurie an admission he has so far refused to make. He tells her, "'Not just in trouble. In what I suppose one would call disgrace'" (83). Bev appears uncomfortable, but Lurie admits that may just be a feeling that he projects onto her. Anyway, she is willing to accept his help and asks no further questions.

Lurie's new-found tolerance extends to his daughter's sexuality. As a fiercely heterosexual man, he has always been uncomfortable with his daughter's lesbianism, but he now wonders about what sex is like when it is purely female. He asks himself, "would he be any happier if the lover were a man?" (84). Perhaps, he thinks, sex between women is inherently purer and less violent than sex between a man and a woman.

In this chapter, his own aging becomes harder for Lurie to deny. Living with Lucy he sees as, "Practise for old age ... Practise for fitting in. Practice for the old folk's home" (84). As he lies awake he reads the letters Byron wrote at thirty-two, fat and middle-aged. Byron writes, "'I have always looked to thirty as the barrier to any real or fierce delight in the passions'" (85). Not for the first time, Lurie reflects on his own aging and on what life might be like when not ruled by the passions.

Disgrace by J.M. Coetzee

Chapter Eleven

Translations

"*basta*" (87) – enough.
"*Hamba!*" (90) – effectively 'Go away!'
"'Hai!'" (93) – in Chinese this means 'cunt' which does seem to fit in this context.
"*coup de grâce*" (93) – the final killing blow or shot to finish off an injured being.

Questions

22. What parallels do you see between the rape Lucy and Lurie's own treatment of Melanie?

23. Lurie is burned and temporarily blinded in one eye. What symbolic significance might the reader find in this? (Clue: In Chapter One Lurie, who considers himself happy, says that "he has not forgotten the last chorus of *Oedipus*: Call no man happy until he is dead" (2). Oedipus, of course, blinds himself at the end of *Oedipus Rex*.)

Commentary

Lurie and Lucy once again discuss his reaction to being dismissed from the university. Lucy accuses him of simple running away rather than stating his case. Lurie finds in this evidence of how Lucy has changed since childhood:

> As a child Lucy had been quiet and self-effacing, observing him but never, as far as he knew, judging him. Now, in her middle twenties, she has begun to separate. The dogs, the gardening, the astrology books, the asexual clothes: in each he recognizes a statement of independence, considered, purposeful. The turn away from men too. Making her own life. Coming out of his shadow. Good! He approves! (86-87)

It is ironic that Lurie here approves of the way his daughter is becoming her own person separate from him because by the end of the chapter they will be far more separate in a way that troubles him deeply. Challenged about the way he has acted, Lurie tells his daughter:

> "The case you want me to make is a case that can no longer be made, basta. Not in our day. If I tried to make it I would not be heard ... My case rests on the rights of desire ... On the god who makes even the small birds quiver." (87)

35

A Study Guide

His argument is that he is being punished for following his instincts, but Lucy questions whether "'men should be allowed to follow their instincts unchecked'" which she finds immoral (88).

The attack and subsequent rape of Lucy suddenly makes this abstract discussion very concrete. Lurie finds himself powerless to help either himself or his daughter; the dogs are also unable to protect them. Instinctively, he stereotypes the attackers as "savages" and himself as "a missionary in a cassock" being put into their "boiling cauldron" (93). This is his racist mindset and it shows that his liberalism is a facade. Even though he speaks English, French and Italian, he cannot understand what his attackers are saying, which exposes the inadequacies of his white Western education to the new realities of South Africa.

In the midst of the incident, when he is locked in the lavatory, Lurie thinks, "So it has come, the day of testing. Without warning, without fanfare, it is here, and he is in the middle of it ... How will they stand up to the testing, he and his heart?" (91-92). Lurie knows that he is facing something greater than he has ever faced in his life – perhaps the defining moment of his life. He feels guilty for not having anticipated the danger of the three men and for not being able to keep his daughter safe from them.

These men have, like him, acted in the perfect tense, "Burned, burnt" (94), in that they carry their desires through to the logical end. He reflects that South Africa is now a country where this "happens every day, every hour, every minute ... in every quarter of the country" (95).

Ironically, he gives the academic theory that explains such violence, "Not human evil, just a vast circulatory system, to whose workings pity and terror are irrelevant. That is how one must see life in this country: in its systematic aspect" (96). Of course, he cannot see what has happened in this way because it has happened to himself and his daughter.

The incident separates father and daughter because of the difference of what they have suffered. Notice that Lucy's first action is to take a bath, "She is wearing a bathrobe, her feet are bare, her hair wet" (94). Recall that after he had forced himself on Melanie, Lurie had "no doubt, she, Melanie, is trying to cleanse herself of it, of him" (23). It is the same reaction. This is why Lucy will not allow her father to touch her when he desperately needs to offer comfort, "[H]e tries to take her in his arms. Gently, decisively, she wriggles loose" (95), and later his efforts to offer her physical comfort by embracing her only show how unresponsive she is, "[He] takes her in his arms. In his embrace she is stiff as a pole, yielding nothing" (97). Father and daughter are divided by gender: he can never know what she has experienced.

Lucy is determined to cover up the fact that she has been raped. She instructs Lurie, "You tell what happened to you, I tell what happened to me"

(96). Lurie (always a man to act on principle) is sure that she is making a big mistake, but she insists.

A Study Guide

Chapter Twelve

Questions

24. What are Lurie's thoughts about Bill Shaw's reaction to the attack on his neighbor?

25. Lurie realizes "that for the second time in a day [Lucy] had spoken to him as if to a child – a child or an old man" (101). Identify the first time this happened.

26. When Lurie asks if her doctor is "'taking care of all eventualities'" following the rape, to what is he referring? Explain why Lucy reacts so strongly to his question.

Commentary

This chapter presents Lurie at his most helpless. On the night following the attack, it is Lucy who takes all of the decisions; he just goes along. By the end of the chapter, Lurie is forced to acknowledge that Lucy is, "Not her father's little girl, not any longer" (103). The fact that Lucy has been raped makes it impossible for him truly to empathize with her or to help her. When he tries, "Bev Shaw responds only with a terse shake of the head. Not your business, she seems to be saying. Menstruation, childbirth, violation and its aftermath: blood-matters; a woman's burden, women's preserve" (102). His view of women who want to live without men has changed radically – perhaps they are right to want to live away from men. He wonders if the men raped Lucy because the word had got around that she is a lesbian.

Lurie also realizes that Lucy no longer defers to him. When he tries to comfort her in the middle of the night, she tells him to go back to sleep, and he realizes "that for the second time in a day she had spoken to him as if to a child – a child or an old man" (101). It happens again when he tries to discover whether Lucy has seen a doctor to ensure that she does not get pregnant or contract a sexually transmitted disease. This is, however, not easy for him to talk about, so he asks her euphemistically whether "'he [her doctor] is taking care of all eventualities?'" Lucy is angered by his assumption that the doctor must be male (a big error since the doctor *he* had seen the previous day was a woman). She has seen a woman. Offended, Lucy tells him, "'No ... how can she? How can a doctor take care of all eventualities? Have some sense!'" (103). For the first time, Lurie shows his irritation: he feels that he is being marginalized by what has happened and he resents it. The huge gulf between the two is clear from their final conversation. Lurie objects to Lucy's plan to go back to the farm because of the danger. She replies, "It was never safe, and it's not an idea, good or bad, I'm not going back for the sake of an idea. I'm just going back" (103). Once again the reader sees the difference between the principled father (who does act "for the sake of" ideas) and the pragmatic daughter.

Chapter Thirteen

Question

27. Explain Lucy's reasons for refusing to report her rape. Do you think she is doing the right thing?

Commentary

We read that, "The events of yesterday have shocked [David] to the core." He has, of course, read of such attacks, but living in Cape Town and working at the university he has been immune from violence. Suddenly, Lurie is confronted by the reality of his age:

> He has a sense that, inside him, a vital organ has been bruised, abused – perhaps even his heart. For the first time he has a taste of what it will be like to be an old man, tired to the bone, without hopes, without desires, indifferent to the future ... His pleasure in living has been snuffed out.

Events since the start of the novel have made him understand his advancing years. He is filled with existential angst, "[H]e has begun to float toward his end ... The blood of life is leaving his body and despair is taking its place..." He knows that Lucy will be relying on him to get things in order and to run the farm, but that is "a burden he is not ready for" (105). Interestingly, although he does not share his terrible psychological wound with Lucy, he does not understand why she is not open and honest about her own wound (i.e., being raped).

Lucy refuses to report the rape to the police – a decision in which Lurie acquiesces only reluctantly because he does not understand it. To him, Lucy seems to be giving her attackers a victory:

> The men will watch the newspapers, listen to the gossip. They will read that they are being sought for robbery and assault and nothing else. It will dawn on them that over the body of the woman silence is being drawn like a blanket. Too ashamed, they will say to each other, too ashamed to tell, and they will chuckle luxuriously, recollecting their exploit. Is Lucy prepared to concede them that victory? (108)

Then Lurie wonders if she is treating what happened as a test of her anti-apartheid convictions. Lucy angrily recognizes their failure to understand one another. She says, "No, you keep misreading me. Guilt and salvation are abstractions. I don't act in terms of abstractions. Until you make the effort to see that I can't help you" (112). Lucy, once again, is a pragmatist. She does not have any expectations of the perpetrators being caught and punished. More fundamentally, she knows that no verbal testimony or punishment will ever be

Disgrace by J.M. Coetzee

adequate reparation for what she has suffered. This is something that she has to deal with on her own terms. Ironically, this situation shows that Lurie's skepticism about the first premise of Communications 101 ("'Human society has created language in order that we may communicate our thoughts, feelings and intentions to each other'" [3]) was right: words are inadequate to some situations; they create not agreement but division.

The reader is aware that Lurie's approach to the rape of his daughter is the very opposite of his response to his own rape of Melanie. He tells Lucy, "It was a crime. There is no shame in being the object of a crime. You did not choose to be the object. You are the innocent party." Now it is Lurie who sees the rape and his daughter's reaction to it in the wider context of the situation in South Africa, while at his hearing he rejected the wider moral context of his action, and it is Lucy who insists that her feelings are "a purely private matter" (109), just as Lurie did at his hearing. Lurie wonders if Lucy is taking this course of action to remind him of "what women undergo at the hands of men" (109) – that is, he wonders if Lucy is trying to imply that he raped Melanie the same way the intruders raped her. Lucy denies this: Lurie is perhaps projecting onto her his new-found awareness of his guilt for what he did.

A Study Guide

Chapter Fourteen

Translations

"*ländliche*" (111) – rural.
"*baas en Klaas*" (114) – boss and worker.
"*paysan*" (115) – peasant, countryman.
"*eingewurzelt*" (115) – deep rooted, deep seated.

Questions

28. Lurie finds himself conflicted about Petrus. What reasons does he have for suspecting the man and what reasons for respecting him?

29. How would Lurie have dealt with Petrus in "the old days," and why can he not do so now? (114).

30. Explain the irony of Lurie insisting that the rape of Lucy was "*a violation ... an outrage*" (117).

Commentary

Lurie, despite his lack of experience, takes over the running of the farm. Lucy is completely introverted. She "keeps to herself, expresses no feelings, shows no interest in anything about her" (112). She says she is not up to going to market, even though she risks losing her stall. Lurie knows it is, "Because of the disgrace. Because of the shame." He bitterly reflects that Lucy is twice a victim: once from the rape and once from the story spread about it by the boasting of the perpetrators, "How they put her in her place, how they showed her what a woman was for" (113). It does not occur to him that his attitude to Melanie was much the same. He does not recall that Melanie did not attend the hearing on the same day he did because she would have had to face her abuser. These parallels probably do occur to the reader.

One thing Lurie does understand is that her daughter's way of life has been destroyed forever. No amount of preparation can ever make the farm safe because they are whites in South Africa – significantly he never uses the word 'apartheid' which is another failure to face the realities of the present situation. Lurie knows that Lucy "is here because she loves the land and the old *landliche* way of life. If that way of life is doomed, what is left for her to love?" (111). Her attackers have taken everything from her.

Lurie is not able to make up his mind about Petrus: on the one hand, he likes and admires the man, but on the other he cannot rid himself of the suspicion that Petrus had some part in the attack on Lucy's farm. When he actually speaks to Petrus about the crime, he says accusingly, "I find it hard to believe the reason [the robbers] picked on us was simply that we were the first white folk they met that day. What do you think? Am I wrong?" (116). If Petrus picks up on the implication, he makes no reaction to it. He remains calm, smoking his pipe, telling Lurie that he is not wrong to want the men brought to justice. This is not enough for Lurie who silently resents Petrus "*weighing [his] words so judiciously.*" What Lurie wants is recognition that what the men did to Lucy was "*a violation ... an outrage*" (117). He seems unaware that in demanding an explicit statement from Petrus that what happened to his daughter "*was a violation ... was an outrage*" (117), he is asking for the very thing he refused to say in his own hearing where Faroldia Rassool objected that "'all of a sudden it is not abuse of a young woman he [Lurie] is confessing to, just an impulse he could not resist...'" (50-51).

Even aside from the attack, Lurie recognizes that the power balance between Lucy and Petrus (and between blacks and white farmers in the area) is fundamentally changing:

> It is a new world they live in, he and Lucy and Petrus. Petrus knows it, and he knows it, and Petrus knows that he knows it ... Petrus will not be content to plough forever his hectare and a half ... Petrus would like to take over Lucy's land ... Petrus has a vision of the future in which people like Lucy have no place. (119)

The university professor who exploited his power over a student now understands what it is like to be vulnerable and powerless.

A Study Guide

Chapter Fifteen

Translation

"regina et imperatrix" (131) – queen and empress (used with reference to Queen Victoria).

Questions

31. Talking to Lurie and Lucy, Petrus says, "No more dogs. I am no longer the dog-man" (126). What point is he making? Where does he make another dig at Lucy?

32. How is Lucy's decision not to telephone the police related to her sense of the changed relations between blacks and whites in post-apartheid South Africa?

33. Do you feel that Petrus was in any way involved in the attack on Lucy's farm by the three men? Explain your reasons.

Commentary

Lurie's personal distaste for the sacrifice of the two lambs is another indication that he has still not accepted the cultural change that has taken place in South Africa. He objects to Petrus "'bringing the slaughter-beasts home to acquaint them with the people who are going to eat them.'" Although he never articulates this idea, perhaps he also sees the lambs as a veiled threat by Petrus about the fate of the remaining whites in the area. Lucy is much more understanding of the way things are done in the African country. This difference is fundamental to the rift that has developed between them. Lurie reflects, "There are spells when the two of them are like strangers in the same house" (121). Initially, Lurie refuses to go to Petrus' party, partly because of the goats but more fundamentally, the reader suspects, because it is to celebrate the land transfer to Petrus. When Lurie finally agrees to go, it is he who notices that he and Lucy "are the only whites" (125); Lucy later joins in with the dancing, while Lurie looks on.

There is an edge of antagonism to everything that Petrus says. When he declares he is, "'not any more the dog-man,'" he is expressing resentment at his former position of subservience and asserting his new status as Lucy's equal. When he responds to Lucy's gift by saying, "'Lucy is our benefactor,'" Lurie finds the word "distasteful ... double-edged, souring the moment" (126). Petrus is mocking the whole white concept of bringing charity to the poor blacks. Again, the resentment is palpable.

Lurie asks Petrus' wife when her baby is due, but "She looks at him uncomprehendingly." Lurie has committed a cultural error by asking Petrus' wife, because a woman cannot speak of such things to a man. Petrus "intervenes" and speaks on her behalf saying how much better it would be to

Disgrace by J.M. Coetzee

have a boy than a girl because, "'Then he can show his sisters. Show them how to behave. Yes.'" It is clear that Petrus is no believer in the equality of the sexes: in his world men rule and women follow, but the reader remembers that this was very much the attitude that Lurie once took to the women he seduced. Petrus makes a partial exception for Lucy who he regards "'as good as a boy. Almost!'" (127). Although he does not say so openly, this is probably a reference to the fact that she is a lesbian, and since Lurie suspects that his daughter's lesbianism might have been a reason for the rape, it is an insensitive thing to say.

When Lucy spies one of her attackers at the party, Lurie confronts the man and a scene ensues. They leave, but Lucy refuses to allow Lurie to call the police because she does not want to ruin Petrus' party. She insists on not taking action until they, "'have heard Petrus' side of the story.'" In response, Lurie accuses her of wanting "'to make up for the wrongs of the past,'" and urges her to stand us for herself (130). He feels that she is being unrealistic in staying on at the farm and in believing that she can co-exist with her black neighbors.

On the whole, this section pivots on the delicate balance between Lurie's personal outrage and Lucy's historical perspective. Coetzee gives no indication which approach is best; he merely presents the dilemma in all its complexity. Lucy feels that, given the political and cultural situation in the country, she must deal with the rape as her business and hers alone while Lurie seeks public vindication (the same vindication that his university hearing was seeking for Melanie). Neither character really understands the other's position; they have become alienated from each other. When Lucy has gone to her room, Lurie reflects:

> Step by step, as inexorably as if they were man and wife, he and she are being driven apart, and there is nothing he can do about it. Their very quarrels have become like the bickerings of a married couple, trapped together with nowhere else to go. (131)

Lurie knows that Lucy has no future on the farm: the days of white farmers living in isolation are over. Perhaps to assert his independence of her, and as a silent protest against the country South Africa has become, Lurie goes back to the party and makes sure that the culprit and the other guests see that he is not afraid to be there.

A Study Guide

Chapter Sixteen

Translations

"*handlanger*" (133) – unskilled assistant.
"kaffir" (137) – an insulting and contemptuous term for a black African.
"*Lösung*," "*lösen*" (139) – to loosen, to detach, to dissolve.
"*muti* shops" (142) – shops that sell remedies based on traditional medicine.
"*harijan*" (143) – a hereditary Hindu group - the lowest socially and spiritually – formerly called the Untouchables.

Questions

34. When he talks to Bev Shaw, Lurie is feeling pretty angry with Petrus. What different view of Lucy's relationship with Petrus does Bev give?

35. What advice does Bev give Lurie about his relationship with Lucy?

36. How does Lurie's role in taking the bodies of dogs to be incinerated further illustrate that he has switched positions with Petrus?

Commentary

When Lurie goes with Petrus to help him to lay pipes to move water to his land, Lurie notes that the traditional relationship of the races is reversed, "His own role at the dam becomes clear. Petrus needs him not for advice on pipefitting or plumbing, but to hold things, to pass him tools – to be his *handlanger*, in fact" (133). Strangely, Lurie has no objection, recognizing Petrus as the superior workman. Lurie's dislike of Petrus goes deeper, it reflects his awareness that as a white man he has lost his power and position: Lurie's education and abstract learning are of no use to him, while Petrus' practical skills are enabling him to build a future by taking over white land. Thus their antagonistic relationship mirrors the historical transfer of power from white to black in post-apartheid South Africa.

Lurie's antipathy becomes clear when he finally asks Petrus about the young man at the party. Petrus' view is that the incident is finished, that the insurance will make good Lurie's losses, and that he can ensure that Lucy will be safe in future. Lurie, however, insists that "'there is a principle involved. We can't just leave it to insurance companies to deliver justice'" (134). Once again the reader notes that Lurie, an idealist, comes into conflict with a realist, a pragmatist. Lurie is even more angry when it becomes clear that Petrus knows that Lucy was raped. Lurie responds ambiguously, "'You know. You know the future? What can I say to that? You have spoken'" (136). So saying, Lurie walks off, but what does he mean? I take him to mean that Petrus know that the future is that white farmers will be pushed out of the Eastern Cape, and that there is nothing they can do about it.

Disgrace by J.M. Coetzee

It adds to Lurie's frustration that Lucy still regards him as not having been there when she was raped, "You weren't there. You don't know what happened." Technically, of course, he was locked in the lavatory, but he is baffled because he feels that he *does* know what rape is. He asks himself, "Do they think he does not know what rape is? ... Or do they think that, where rape is concerned, no man can be where the woman is?" This is obviously ironic given that the reader might consider Lurie to have raped Melanie, a word that he explicitly rejected at the time. (See page 23.) He feels himself "outraged, outraged at being treated like an outsider" (137).

Lurie spends his time at the Animal Welfare clinic. He takes responsibility for delivering the bodies of euthanized dogs to the incinerator and for ensuring that their bones are not broken when they are loaded into the incinerator. Reflecting on why this is so important to him he concludes that he does it, "For himself ... For his idea of the world, a world in which men do not use shovels to beat corpses into a more convenient shape for processing ... He saves the honor of the corpses because there is no one else stupid enough to do it" (142-143). Sherrod writes:

> Lurie responds to the overwhelming pressure of these complex questions by developing sympathy for animals. It is almost as though he displaces the grief and shame he won't allow himself to express about the rapes of Melanie and his daughter onto a simple affection for the dogs he must kill and bury. (Gradesaver, Chapters 16-20)

Whatever he has said earlier, it is hard not to see his action as a form of reparation for his crime against Melanie.

A Study Guide

Chapter Seventeen

Questions

37. Lurie has sex with Bev Shaw. Are you surprised? Shocked?

38. How does Lurie feel about himself at the end of this chapter?

Commentary

What happens in this chapter probably comes as a shock, and probably leaves the reader confused. On the one hand, Lurie admits to Bev, "'Yes, there was a woman involved. But I was the troublemaker in that case. I caused the young woman in question at least as much trouble as she caused me'" (144). This is further than he has ever gone before in admitting his responsibility. On the other hand, he still insists that he did not regret what he was doing at the time. He tells Bev, "'In the heat of the act there are no doubts'" (145).

His reaction to having sex with Bev (whose husband responded so supportively after the attack) is problematic. He sees her as having made careful preparations which, of course, pushes responsibility for what happens onto Bev. He says she, "thinks, because he comes from the big city, that he makes love to many women and expects to be made love to by every woman who crosses his path" (146). This seems to be an example of projecting his own view of himself onto Bev. Nevertheless, the sex is certainly consensual, so the affair has none of the elements of coercion that were evident in his pursuit of Melanie.

The reality of his age strikes Lurie when he sees his own "bowed shoulders and skinny shanks. It is indeed late." That second sentence shows he is aware of his own aging, and he falls into self-pity, reflecting, "This is what I have to get used to. This and even less than this." He tells himself to "stop calling her poor Bev Shaw. If she is poor, he is bankrupt" (147). There is a new humility here.

Disgrace by J.M. Coetzee

Chapter Eighteen

Translation

"*Sunt lacrimae rerum, et mentem mortalia tangunt*" (159) – There are tears, and human sorrows.

Questions

39. Explain why Lucy refuses to leave the farm even for a little while.

40. What is more fundamental for Lucy in considering the rape she suffered, the race or the gender of her attackers? Explain your answer.

Commentary

Lurie sees his daughter as having "been outplayed on all fronts" by Petrus who "arrived as the dig-man, the carry-man, the water-man" and is now too busy to do those jobs (148). Lurie sees that the old South Africa has gone forever. Men like Petrus are now in control, men who work for their own advancement not that of their white overseers. This is confirmed for Lurie when Petrus turns down the idea of managing Lucy's farm while she takes a holiday. To Petrus, the term "'farm manager'" (149) is a degrading reminder of the old days of apartheid. Notice how he repeats the word "must" when he outlines what he would be required to do as farm manager; he is making the point that the days when white people tell him what to do are past.

The car that the police claim to have recovered turns out not to be the right car – another example of the ineffectiveness of the police in the new South Africa. However, on the way home, Lucy does finally open up to Lurie about the rape. She tells him, "It was so personal. It was done with such personal hatred. That was what stunned me more than anything. The rest was ... expected. But why did they hate me so? I had never set eyes on them." Lurie tries to put the hatred into an historical perspective which, he hopes, will depersonalize it for Lucy. He replies, "It was history speaking through them ... A history of wrong. Think of it that way if it helps. It may have seemed personal, but it wasn't. It came down from the ancestors" (153). Lucy makes the point that knowing the background does not help her to come to terms with a man hating her at the moment of intercourse.

Lurie tries to persuade Lucy that he does understand what she went through. He even reveals his own sense of guilt for not having been there to protect her, "'And I did nothing. I did not save you.' That was his own confession" (154). She tells him to stop blaming himself for failing to protect her because that is not the core of the problem for Lucy. This proves to be what the incident has taught her about the role of men and women in the sexual act. She speculates, "'Maybe, for men, hating the woman makes sex more exciting. You are a man, you ought to know. When you have sex with someone strange – when you trap her, hold her down, get her under you, put all your weight on her

– isn't it a bit like killing?'" Lurie recognizes that the fact that he is a man stands between them: she is describing his own seductions in the same terms as her being raped. Perhaps to distract from this painful truth, he returns to the racial aspects of the crime telling Lucy, "'If they had been white you wouldn't talk about them in this way'" (155). Lucy is doubtful, but even recognizing that the three men who raped her wanted "'Subjugation. Subjugation'" because she was white, she refuses to leave the farm (156).

All of Lurie's academic knowledge of rape is suddenly irrelevant. Even Byron, who surely did commit rape, is "very old fashioned indeed." If he tries really hard, Lurie can think himself into the minds of the men who committed this violation, but the more important question is, "does he have it in him to be the woman?" (156). Even to ask this question shows that he has come a long way from the man who abused Melanie.

Disgrace by J.M. Coetzee

Chapter Nineteen

Questions

41. Several surprising things happen in this chapter: Lurie goes to visit the Isaacs; Mr. Isaacs invites him to dinner; and Lurie offers an apology. None of this is explained. How would you explain the motivation of both Lurie and Isaacs?

42. As he is attempting to leave, Isaacs says to Lurie, "'Yes, you came to speak to me, but why me? ... So who did you really come to speak to?'" (169). Lurie feels that he does not like Isaacs, "does not like his tricks" (170). Explain what you think Isaacs means and why Lurie reacts as he does.

Commentary

Lurie tells Mr. Isaacs that he wishes to "'say what is on my heart,'" but it seems that all he does is give his side of the story – a defense of sorts. He tells Isaacs that his relationship with Melanie began as another in a string of "'little adventures'" (162) but that, "'In Melanie's case, however, something unexpected happened. I think of it as a fire. She struck up a fire in me ... a flame-god. It was that kind of flame your daughter kindled in me'" (163). This seems to be going back to his defense at his hearing: a defense based on the impulse of desire. The closest he comes to admitting to himself that he raped Melanie is when he remembers that he put whisky in her coffee "that was intended to – the word comes up reluctantly – *lubricate* her" (165). 'Lubricate' is a euphemism for 'make her compliant.' This is perhaps what he means when he admits to Isaacs "'I manage love too well'" (168).

He does, finally, offer Mr. Isaacs an apology, "'I am sorry for what I took your daughter through ... I apologize for the grief I have caused you and Mrs. Isaacs. I ask for pardon.'" Nevertheless, he is still defensive, claiming that his relationship with Melanie "'could have turned out differently ... despite our ages. But there was something I failed to supply, something ... lyrical. I lack the lyrical'" (168). He is still claiming that there was something more than physical in the relationship, at least on his part. However, during his visits to the Isaac home, Lurie does find himself reacting sexually to the beautiful younger sister Desiree. For example, he fantasizes about, "The two of them in the same bed: an experience fit for a king" (161), and when he looks into her eyes "again the current leaps, the current of desire" (170). Lurie seems to have learned nothing from his experiences. When Isaacs asks, "'So who did you really come to speak to?'" (169), Lurie feels tricked. Surely the answer is that he came in the hope of seeing Melanie and of persuading her to reignite their affair.

Chapter Twenty

Translations

"*Aliter*" (175) – otherwise – "frequently used to point out a difference between two decisions; as, a point of law has been decided in a particular way, in such a case, aliter in another case" (TheFreeDictionary).
"*reliquie*" (177) – relics.
"*contadina*" (177) – peasant woman.

Question

43. Why is Lurie so drawn to the subject of Byron's last years in Italy? With what in Byron's experience does he relate?

Commentary

When Lurie returns to Cape Town, he notices that in less than three months the shanty settlements have grown and that there are more animals about. Fatalistically, he concludes, "the country is coming to the city ... soon history will have come full circle" (171). Presumably he means that the native black population will have taken over from the colonizing white population. He finds that his home has been burgled and everything of value taken and reflects that it is one more example of "war reparations; another incident in the great campaign of redistribution" (172).

Although he has obviously looked forward to returning to the civilization of Cape Town, he finds himself to be a stranger with no connection to his past life. His home has been trashed; Dr. Otto, a "young man" (173), has taken possession of his office; in "the little shop where for years he has bought his coffee the assistant pretends not to recognize him"; "his neighbour, watering her garden, studiously keeps her back turned" (174); and he has a chilly encounter with Elaine Winter, chair of his old department, in the supermarket. There is nothing of his old life there anymore.

Finally he makes progress on his Byron opera, but it evolves very differently from the way he planned it. It will not be the tale of the passionate young Contessa Guiccioli trying to stir a Byron who was "once passionate but now [is a] less passionate older man" (176). Lurie has to admit that "the project has failed to engage the core of him" (177). Instead, he imagines Guiccioli in middle-age trying to call back the long-dead Byron. Lurie's Byron wants to remain dead while Teresa must repossess him in order to relive the one passion that made her life meaningful. Lurie has a moment of epiphany, "That is what Soraya and the others were for: to suck the complex proteins out of his blood like snake-venom, leaving him clear-headed and dry" (181). Then there comes the sound of another voice, Allegra, Byron's dying daughter who asks, "Why have you forgotten me?" (182).

Disgrace by J.M. Coetzee

How does this relate to Lurie's life and situation? It seems that instead of identifying himself with the middle-aged Byron, Lurie identifies with Teresa unavailingly trying to recapture a passion that has died. It also reminds him that he too has forgotten his daughter, who surely deserves his love.

Chapter Twenty-one

Translations
"*contra naturam*" (186) – against nature.
"*Kaaps*" (187) – Cape.
"*jou dom meid!*" (188) – you stupid girl!
"*Omnis gens quaecumque se in se perficere vult*" (190) – Every nation, whatever it is, wishes to perfect itself in itself.

Questions
44. Why do you think that Lurie goes to see the play that Melanie is performing in? What does he learn from the experience?

45. Lurie has sex with a prostitute. What does he learn from the experience?

Commentary
Rosalind calls Lurie and they meet over coffee. Lurie's first memories of her are of their steamy sex, "sheets damp with perspiration, Rosalind's long, pale body thrashing this way and that in the throes of a pleasure that was hard to tell from pain" (183). To his claim that at his university hearing he was "'standing up for a principle ... Freedom of speech. Freedom to remain silent,'" she replies that he has always been "'[a] great deceiver and a great self-deceiver.'" A realist herself, she tells him that he surely should "'know by now that tribunals are not about principles, they are about how well you put yourself across'" (184). Although he rejects the idea, she warns him that he has lost everything and faces a degrading future. This encounter gives the reader another realistic alternative to Lurie's romanticized version of events.

Rosalind's mention of Melanie "unsettles" Lurie. He feels again that there was "something unfinished" in their affair. He thinks that his dismissal was all about stopping an old man from performing "unnatural acts" with a young woman. Yet at the same time he knows that trying to reconnect with Melanie is "crazy" (186). Realistically, since the attack, his looks are odd and unattractive. His attempt to see her in the play at the Dock Theater ends in another confrontation with her boyfriend. Lurie's dreams that his encounters with women have "Enriched" his life, and his romantic view that "they too are plunged without warning into the ocean of memory" where they recall him, is contrasted with the reality of the boyfriend's warning that "'Melanie will spit in your eye if she sees you,'" and by the ease with which Lurie picks up a prostitute. He reflects, "*So this is all it takes! ... How could I ever have forgotten it?*" He takes the prostitute back where she came from. For Lurie, this is a "*night of revelations*" (190). It seems that he has got over his tendency to idealize and romanticize sex.

Disgrace by J.M. Coetzee

Chapter Twenty-two

Translations

"Ovral" (193) - a contraceptive in tablet form used to prevent pregnancy.
"'*bywonder*'" (199) – a poor tenant farmer.

Questions

46. Explain why Lucy has not taken action to prevent a pregnancy or to terminate the pregnancy.

47. Why do you think that Lucy accepts Petrus' offer of marriage? What conditions does she make?

Commentary

When Lurie discovers that Lucy is pregnant, he cannot believe that she has not sought an abortion. He asks why she has not told him earlier and Lucy replies:

> "You behave as if everything I do is part of the story of your life. You are the main character, I am a minor character who doesn't make an appearance until halfway through. Well, contrary to what you think, people are not divided into major and minor. I am not a minor. I have a life of my own, just as important to me as yours is to you, and in my life I am the one who makes the decisions." (193)

Lucy insists that she will have the baby because she is a woman. She reveals that she has already had one abortion and has no intention of putting herself through another. Lurie has to accept that he has, up to this point, had an entirely self-centered approach to life.

Lurie's confrontation with Petrus comes down to a racial clash. Petrus will defend his "people," his relative Pollux, and Lurie will defend his "people," his daughter. Lurie insists that what has happened to Lucy is part of a racial clash that will intensify in South Africa, "'It is not finished. Don't pretend you don't know what I mean. It is not finished. On the contrary, it is just beginning. It will go on long after I am dead and you are dead'" (196). Lurie reacts with shock to Petrus' proposal that he (who already has two wives) should marry Lucy to ensure her safety since a marriage would make her part of his extended family. Lurie replies, "'This is not how we do things.' *We*: he is on the point of saying, *We Westerners*" (197). The clash of cultures is also a clash of temperaments: Lurie, the man of ideals and principles, despite all of his affairs believes in monogamy, while Petrus, the pragmatist, believes in doing what will make Lucy safe and advantage himself.

Once again, reality has broken in on Lurie's dreams. Lucy accepts Petrus' offer of 'marriage' (with clear conditions) because she knows that she has no choice: it is the only way she can stay safely on the land, and she will not leave the land. Rejecting Lurie's proposals that she leave, she tells him "'to consider [her] situation objectively ... Practically speaking, there is only Petrus left" (199). They both agree that the arrangement with Petrus will be humiliating, but Lucy adds:

> "[I]t is humiliating. But perhaps that is a good point to start from again. Perhaps this what I must learn to accept. To start at ground level. With nothing. Not with nothing but. With nothing. No cards, no weapons, no property, no rights, no dignity."
> "Like a dog."
> "Yes, like a dog." (200)

Lurie, however, still cannot take the humiliation; he remains a man of principle.

Disgrace by J.M. Coetzee

Chapter Twenty-three

Translations

"*Du musst dein Leben ändern!*" (204) – a translation is given immediately after this quotation in the text.

"*Vedi l'anime di color cui vinse l'ira*" (204) – Now see the souls of those who anger has defeated (a reference to Dante's poem *The Divine Comedy*).

Question

48. In this chapter, for the first time, practicality overweighs principle in Lurie's motivation. Give some examples.

Commentary

When Lurie sees Pollux looking in on Lucy through the bathroom window, he sets Katy on the boy and beats him. For the first time, Lurie gives in to "elemental rage. He would like to give the boy what he deserves: a sound thrashing. "Phrases that all his life he has avoided seem suddenly just right: *Teach him a lesson, Show him his place*. So this is what it is like, he thinks! This is what it is like to be a savage!" (201). The cultured university professor has finally been revealed (to himself) as a racist bigot. He reflects that, "he is too old to heed, too old to change. Lucy may be able to bend to the tempest; he cannot, not with honour" (204). Still he insists on living his life by principles.

When he meets Bev at the clinic, "They embrace, tentative as strangers. Hard to believe they once lay naked in each other's arms" (204). She tells him that Lucy is more adaptable to the changing situation in the country than he is because she is younger and because "'Women are adaptable.'" Thus, Lurie feels alienated from his daughter both by his gender and his age, but this time he takes Bev's advice "'to stand back and let Lucy work out solutions for herself'" (205). For the first time, he stops trying to run his daughter's life. He goes back to helping Bev to euthanize the dogs and taking them to the incinerator, for which purpose he buys a truck. This leads to the most important of the several epiphanies he has had in the course of the narrative: he reflects that the old truck "does not have to last forever. Nothing has to last forever" – which is a very pragmatic way of looking at things (206).

A Study Guide

Chapter Twenty-four

Translations

"'*Che vuol dir ... Che vuol dir questa solitudine immensa: Ed io ... che sono?*'" (208) – "What does this mean / Immense loneliness? And what am I?" (G. Leopardi – "Night song of an errant Shepherd of Asia").
"Driepoot" (210) – Tripod (because he only has three legs).
"*das ewig Weibliche*" (213) – the eternal feminine.

Questions

49. Lurie has to admit "that Byron in Italy is going nowhere. There is no action, no development" (209). Explain why the opera, as Lurie now conceived it, cannot move forward but must constantly repeat itself. What exactly does it repeat?
50. Lurie composes the music for his opera on a banjo and considers including a part for a dog (210). What significance do you find in these two details?
51. In what sense does Lucy's unborn child represent transition?

Commentary

He continues to play with his opera but he now recognizes it as "a work that will never be performed" (210). His hopes for it "must be more temperate" – he hopes that he will capture just "a single authentic note of immortal longing" (109).

When he goes to visit Lucy, he thinks for the first time of the prospect of being a grandfather. Initially, he thinks he will do no better job as a grandfather than he has done as a father, but then he is honest, "He lacks the virtues of the old: equanimity, kindliness, patience. But perhaps those virtues will come as other virtues go: the virtue of passion, for instance ... There may be things to learn." There is a new humility here. He reflects that his family line will go on, "a line of existences in which his share, his gift, will grow inexorably less and less, till it may as well be forgotten" (212). This sounds like a man who has come to terms with his own mortality. Earlier Lurie had thought of himself as, "A father without the sense to have a son: is this how it is all going to end, is this how his line is going to run out, like water dribbling into the earth?" (194). He has come a long way since he thought that: he has accepted the child in Lucy's womb as his issue, and he has accepted the role of grandfather.

Lucy offers him tea, as she would any visitor, and he reflects, "She makes the offer as if he were a visitor. Good. Visitorship, visitation: a new footing, a new start" (213). The two are beginning an entirely new relationship – one in which they are equals. Lurie has learned that he has no right to micro-manage the life of his adult daughter's life. His final act of realism is to bring to be euthanized his favorite dog. In answer to Bev's question, he says, "'Yes, I am giving him up'" (215). The only real clue to Lurie's motivation is his earlier

Disgrace by J.M. Coetzee

thought that the dog's "period of grace is almost over; soon it will have to submit to the needle" (210). The narrator leaves it entirely to the reader to make sense of Lurie's action. Is he saving the dog from disgrace (the disgrace he has himself suffered)? In killing the injured dog is he, in some sense, killing his own former self – his disgraced self? Does the dog represent white people in the Eastern Cape whose time has come? The narrator is silent.

There is plenty of evidence in the text to support the idea that the ending is negative. Sherrod puts the case admirably:

> [H]is line will be carried on through hatred, violence and accident. Neither Lurie's nor Lucy's hope for the future is positive ... In the midst of this desolate, perpetual tragedy, Lurie and Lucy – two South African whites who couldn't be more different – can find meaning only in disgrace. Lucy accepts a humiliating position as Petrus' third wife or concubine in exchange for protection, for the privilege of living out her years on the land she loves. Lurie, incapable of redeeming himself for crimes that seem to follow from his very being, resigns himself to bringing dignity to dead dogs. Each shoulders his or her disgrace, resigned to live for small private satisfactions in a wounded nation.

This is a powerful reading, but I should like to offer an alternative: the world is imperfect and our lives are temporary, and within those parameters we do the best we can with what we have got to work with. That is what Lucy has always been flexible enough to do. The personal triumph of the novel is that Lurie, the man who has tried to live inflexibly by ideals and principles finds the strength to join her on her journey through life.

Perspectives

Consider the following comments on the novel – ideally in discussion.

[The] characterization of violence by both the 'white' and the 'black' man parallels feelings in post-apartheid South Africa where evil does not belong to the 'other' alone ... The novel takes its inspiration from South Africa's contemporary social and political conflict, and offers a bleak look at a country in transition. (Wikipedia article)

The novel avoids preaching or over-sentimentalizing any form of conversion he appears to have undergone, but it is nevertheless finally optimistic about how others (namely David) can continue learning as they grow older. (Novelguide)

Disgrace by J.M. Coetzee

Annotated Works Cited:

"Disgrace". Novelguide. Web. 2 May 2017.
 (A useful site, but heavy on summary.)

Sherrod, Cheryl. Miller, W.C. ed. "Disgrace" by J. M. Coetzee. *GradeSaver*, 26 October 2006 Web. 10 April 2017.
 (I found this site to be extremely useful, not least because I frequently disagreed with its interpretation.)

Shmoop Editorial Team. "Disgrace" by J. M. Coetzee. *Shmoop*. Shmoop University, Inc., 11 Nov. 2008. Web. 2 May 2017.
 (The most useful section (as always) was "Analysis.")

Wikipedia contributors. "Disgrace". *Wikipedia*, The Free Encyclopedia. Wikipedia, The Free Encyclopedia, 1 Mar. 2017. Web. 1 May 2017.
 (Brief but helpful.)

A Study Guide

Literary terms

Allegorical: a story in which the characters, their actions and the settings represent abstract ideas (often moral ideas) or historical/political events.

Ambiguous, ambiguity: when a statement is unclear in meaning – ambiguity may be deliberate or accidental.

Analogy: a comparison which treats two things as identical in one or more specified ways.

Antagonist: a character or force opposing the protagonist.

Antithesis: the complete opposite of something.

Authorial comment: when the writer addresses the reader directly (not to be confused with the narrator doing so).

Climax: the conflict to which the action has been building since the start of the play or story.

Colloquialism: the casual, informal mainly spoken language of ordinary people – often called "slang."

Connotation: the ideas, feelings and associations generated by a word or phrase.

Dark comedy: comedy which has a serious implication – comedy that deals with subjects not usually treated humorously (e.g., death).

Dialogue: a conversation between two or more people in direct speech.

Diction: the writer's choice of words in order to create a particular effect.

Equivocation: saying something which is capable of two interpretations with the intention of misrepresenting the truth.

Euphemism: a polite word for an ugly truth – for example, a person is said to be sleeping when they are actually dead.

Fallacy: a misconception resulting from incorrect reasoning.

Foreshadow: a statement or action which gives the reader a hint of what is likely to happen later in the narrative.

Genre: the type of literature into which a particular text falls (e.g. drama, poetry, novel).

Hubris: pride – in Greek tragedy it is the hero's belief that he can challenge the will of the gods.

Hyperbole: exaggeration designed to create a particular effect.

Disgrace by J.M. Coetzee

Image, imagery: figurative language such as simile, metaphor, personification etc., or a description which conjures up a particularly vivid picture.

Imply, implication: when the text suggests to the reader a meaning which it does not actually state.

Infer, inference: the reader's act of going beyond what is stated in the text to draw conclusions.

Irony, ironic: a form of humor which undercuts the apparent meaning of a statement:

> *Conscious irony:* irony used deliberately by a writer or character;
> *Unconscious irony:* a statement or action which has significance for the reader of which the character is unaware;
> *Dramatic irony*: when an action has an important significance that is obvious to the reader but not to one or more of the characters;
> *Tragic irony:* when a character says (or does) something which will have a serious, even fatal, consequence for him/ her. The audience is aware of the error, but the character is not;
> *Verbal irony*: the conscious use of particular words which are appropriate to what is being said.

Juxtaposition: literally putting two things side by side for purposes of comparison and/ or contrast.

Literal: the surface level of meaning that a statement has.

Melodramatic: action and/or dialogue that is inflated or extravagant – frequently used for comic effect.

Metaphor, metaphorical: the description of one thing by direct comparison with another (e.g. the coal-black night).

> *Extended metaphor:* a comparison which is developed at length.

Microcosm: literally 'the world is little' – a situation which reflects truths about the world in general.

Mood: the feelings and emotions contained in and/ or produced by a work of art (text, painting, music, etc.).

Motif: a frequently repeated idea, image or situation in a text.

Motivation: why a character acts as he/she does – in modern literature motivation is seen as psychological.

Narrator: the voice that the reader hears in the text – not to be confused with the author.

A Study Guide

Oxymoron: the juxtaposition of two terms normally thought of as opposite (e.g. the silent scream).

Paradox, paradoxical: a statement or situation which appears self-contradictory and therefore absurd.

Pathos: is pity, or rather the ability of a text to make the audience or reader feel pity.

Perspective: point of view from which a story, or an incident within a story, is told.

Personified, personification: a simile or metaphor in which an inanimate object or abstract idea is described by comparison with a human.

Plot: a chain of events linked by cause and effect.

Prologue: an introduction which gives a lead-in to the main story.

Protagonist: the character who initiates the action and is most likely to have the sympathy of the audience.

Pun: a deliberate play on words where a particular word has two or more meanings both appropriate in some way to what is being said.

Realism: a text that describes the action in a way that appears to reflect life.

Rhetoric: any use of language designed to make the expression of ideas more effective (e.g. repetition, imagery, alliteration, etc.).

Sarcasm: stronger than irony – it involves a deliberate attack on a person or idea with the intention of mocking.

Satire, Satiric: the use of comedy to criticize attack, belittle, or humiliate – more extreme than irony.

Setting: the environment in which the narrative (or part of the narrative) takes place.

Simile: a description of one thing by explicit comparison with another (e.g. my love is like a red, red rose).

    Extended simile: a comparison which is developed at length.

Style: the way in which a writer chooses to express him/ herself. Style is a vital aspect of meaning since how something is expressed can crucially affect what is being written or spoken.

Suspense: the building of tension in the reader.

Symbol, symbolic, symbolism, symbolize: a physical object which comes to represent an abstract idea (e.g. the sun may symbolize life).

Disgrace by J.M. Coetzee

Themes: important concepts, beliefs and ideas explored and presented in a text.

Third person: third person singular is "he/ she/ it" and plural is "they" – authors often write novels in the third person.

Tone: literally the sound of a text – How words sound (either in the mouth of an actor or the head of a reader) can crucially affect meaning/

Tragic: King Richard III and Macbeth are both murderous tyrants, yet only Macbeth is a *tragic* figure. Why? Because Macbeth has the potential to be great, recognizes the error he has made and all that he has lost in making it, and dies bravely in a way that seems to accept the justice of the punishment

.

Literary terms Activity

As you use each term in the study guide, fill in the definition of the term and include an example from the text to show how it is used. The first definition is supplied. Find an example in the text to complete it.

Term	Definition
	Example
Euphemism	*a polite word for an ugly truth – for example, a person is said to be sleeping when they are actually dead.*
Foreshadow	
Irony. ironic	
Mood	
Motivation/ motivate	

Disgrace by J.M. Coetzee

Term	Definition
	Example
Narrator	
Protagonist	
Symbol/ symbolic/ symbolism/ symbolize	
Third person	

Appendix 1: How I Used the Study Guide Questions

Although there are both closed and open questions in the Study Guide, very few of them have simple, right or wrong answers. They are designed to encourage in-depth discussion, disagreement, and (eventually) consensus. Above all, they aim to encourage students to go to the text to support their conclusions and interpretations.

I am not so arrogant as to presume to tell teachers how they should use this resource. I used it in the following ways, each of which ensured that students were well prepared for class discussion and presentations.

1. Set a reading assignment for the class and tell everyone to be aware that the questions will be the focus of whole class discussion the next class.

2. Set a reading assignment for the class and allocate particular questions to sections of the class (e.g. if there are four questions, divide the class into four sections, etc.).
In class, form discussion groups containing one person who has prepared each question and allow time for feedback within the groups.
Have feedback to the whole class on each question by picking a group at random to present their answers and to follow up with class discussion.

3. Set a reading assignment for the class, but do not allocate questions.
In class, divide students into groups and allocate to each group one of the questions related to the reading assignment the answer to which they will have to present formally to the class.
Allow time for discussion and preparation.

4. Set a reading assignment for the class, but do not allocate questions.
In class, divide students into groups and allocate to each group one of the questions related to the reading assignment. Allow time for discussion and preparation.
Now reconfigure the groups so that each group contains at least one person who has prepared each question and allow time for feedback within the groups.

5. Before starting to read the text, allocate specific questions to individuals or pairs. (It is best not to allocate all questions to allow for other approaches and variety. One in three questions or one in four seems about right.) Tell students that they will be leading the class discussion on their question. They will need to start with a brief presentation of the issues and then conduct a question and answer session. After this, they will be expected to present a brief review of the discussion.

Disgrace by J.M. Coetzee

6. Having finished the text, arrange the class into groups of 3, 4 or 5. Tell each group to select as many questions from the Study Guide as there are members of the group.

Each individual is responsible for drafting out a written answer to one question, and each answer should be a substantial paragraph.

Each group as a whole is then responsible for discussing, editing and suggesting improvements to each answer, which is revised by the original writer and brought back to the group for a final proof reading followed by revision.

This seems to work best when the group knows that at least some of the points for the activity will be based on the quality of all of the answers.

Graphic Organizer- plot

Plot graph

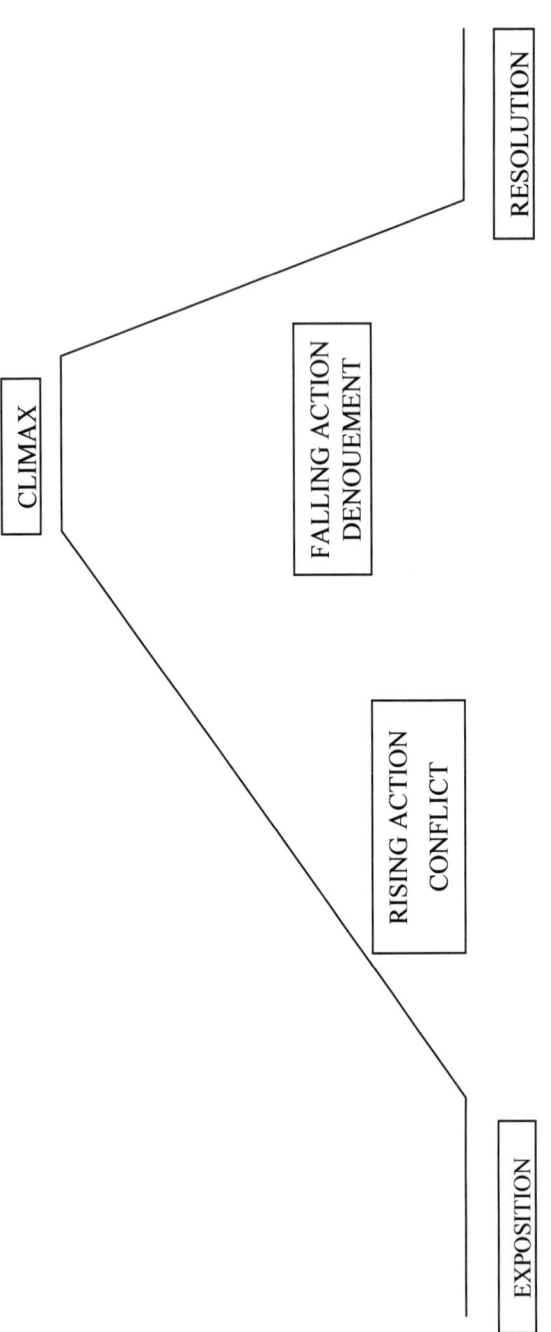

70

Disgrace by J.M. Coetzee

To the Reader

Ray strives to make his texts the best that they can be. If you have any comments or question about this book *please* contact the author through his email: **moore.ray1@yahoo.com**
Visit his website http://www.raymooreauthor.com

Also by Ray Moore:

Books are available as paperbacks and some from online eBook retailers.
Fiction:
The Lyle Thorne Mysteries
Each book features five mysteries from the Golden Age of Detection:
  Investigations of The Reverend Lyle Thorne
  Further Investigations of The Reverend Lyle Thorne
  Early Investigations of Lyle Thorne
  Sanditon Investigations of The Reverend Lyle Thorne
  Final Investigations of The Reverend Lyle Thorne
  Lost Investigations of The Reverend Lyle Thorne
Non-fiction:
The ***Critical Introduction series***
This is written for high school teachers and students and for college undergraduates. Each volume gives an in-depth analysis of a key text:
  "The Stranger" by Albert Camus: A Critical Introduction (Revised Second Edition)
  "The General Prologue" by Geoffrey Chaucer: A Critical Introduction
  "Pride and Prejudice" by Jane Austen: A Critical Introduction
  "The Great Gatsby" by F. Scott Fitzgerald: A Critical Introduction
The Text and Critical Introduction series
This differs from the Critical introduction series as these books contain the original text and in the case of the medieval texts an interlinear translation to aid the understanding of the text. The commentary allows the reader to develop a deeper understanding of the text and themes within the text.
  "Sir Gawain and the Green Knight": Text and Critical Introduction
  "The General Prologue" by Geoffrey Chaucer: Text and Critical Introduction
  "The Wife of Bath's Prologue and Tale" by Geoffrey Chaucer: Text and Critical Introduction
  "Heart of Darkness" by Joseph Conrad: Text and Critical Introduction
  "The Sign of Four" by Sir Arthur Conan Doyle Text and Critical Introduction
  "A Room with a View" By E.M. Forster: Text and Critical Introduction
  "Oedipus Rex" by Sophocles: Text and Critical Introduction
  "Henry V" by William Shakespeare: Text and Critical Introduction

A Study Guide

Study guides - listed alphabetically by author
* denotes also available as an eBook
NOTE Amazon has recently required Study Guides to reflect the nature of the book so eBooks are titled "Study Guide on ...."

"ME and EARL and the Dying GIRL" by Jesse Andrews: A Study Guide

"Pride and Prejudice" by Jane Austen: A Study Guide

"Moloka'i" by Alan Brennert: A Study Guide

"Wuthering Heights" by Emily Brontë: A Study Guide *

"Jane Eyre" by Charlotte Brontë: A Study Guide *

"The Myth of Sisyphus" by Albert Camus: A Study Guide

"The Stranger" by Albert Camus: A Study Guides

"The Myth of Sisyphus" and "The Stranger" by Albert Camus: Two Study Guides *

Study Guide to "Death Comes for the Archbishop" by Willa Cather

"The Awakening" by Kate Chopin: A Study Guide

"The Meursault Investigation" by Kamel Daoud: A Study Guide

"Great Expectations" by Charles Dickens: A Study Guide *

"The Sign of Four" by Sir Arthur Conan Doyle: A Study Guide *

"The Wasteland, Prufrock and Poems" by T.S. Eliot: A Study Guide

"The Great Gatsby" by F Scott Fitzgerald: A Study Guide

"A Room with a View" by E. M. Forster: A Study Guide

"Looking for Alaska" by John Green: A Study Guide

"Paper Towns" by John Green: A Study Guide

"Catch-22" by Joseph Heller: A Study Guide *

"Unbroken" by Laura Hillenbrand: A Study Guide

"The Kite Runner" by Khaled Hosseini: A Study Guide

"A Thousand Splendid Suns" by Khaled Hosseini: A Study Guide

"Go Set a Watchman" by Harper Lee: A Study Guide

"On the Road" by Jack Keruoac: A Study Guide

"Life of Pi" by Yann Martel: A Study Guide *

Study Guide on "The Invention of Wings" by Sue Monk Kidd

"The Secret Life of Bees" by Sue Monk Kidd: A Study Guide

Study Guide to "The Bluest Eye" by Toni Morrison

"Esperanza Rising" by Pam Munoz Ryan: A Study Guide

"Animal Farm" by George Orwell: A Study Guide

Disgrace by J.M. Coetzee
Study Guide on "Nineteen Eight-Four" by George Orwell
"Selected Poems" by Sylvia Plath: A Study Guide *
"An Inspector Calls" by J.B. Priestley: A Study Guide
"The Catcher in the Rye" by J.D. Salinger: A Study Guide
"Where'd You Go, Bernadette" by Maria Semple: A Study Guide
"Henry V" by William Shakespeare: A Study Guide
Study Guide on "Macbeth" by William Shakespeare
"Othello" by William Shakespeare: A Study Guide *
"Antigone" by Sophocles: A Study Guide *
"Oedipus Rex" by Sophocles: A Study Guide
"Cannery Row" by John Steinbeck: A Study Guide
"East of Eden" by John Steinbeck: A Study Guide
*"Of Mice and Men" by John Steinbeck: A Study Guide**
"The Grapes of Wrath" by John Steinbeck: A Study Guide
"The Goldfinch" by Donna Tartt: A Study Guide
"Walden; or, Life in the Woods" by Henry David Thoreau: A Study Guide
Study Guide to "Cat's Cradle" by Kurt Vonnegut
"The Bridge of San Luis Rey" by Thornton Wilder: A Study Guide *
A Study Guide on "The Book Thief" by Markus Zusak

Study Guides available as e-books:
A Study Guide on "Heart of Darkness" by Joseph Conrad:
A Study Guide on "The Mill on the Floss" by George Eliot
A Study Guide on "Lord of the Flies" by William Golding
A Study Guide on "Nineteen Eighty-Four" by George Orwell
A Study Guide on "Henry IV Part 2" by William Shakespeare
A Study Guide on "Julius Caesar" by William Shakespeare
A Study Guide on "The Pearl" by John Steinbeck
A Study Guide on "Slaughterhouse-Five" by Kurt Vonnegut

New titles are added regularly.

Teacher resources:
Ray also publishes many more study guides and other resources for classroom use on the 'Teachers Pay Teachers' website:
http://www.teacherspayteachers.com/Store/Raymond-Moore

Printed in Dunstable, United Kingdom